Financing Community Colleges

Walter I. Garms

Teachers College Press
Teachers College, Columbia University
New York, New York

Library of Congress Cataloging in Publication Data
Garms, Walter I
  Financing community colleges.

  Bibliography: p.
  1. Community colleges—United States—Finance.
I. Title.
LB2328.G28   378'.052·   76-54165
ISBN 0-8077-2510-2

Manufactured in the United States of America

Designed by Frank Medina

Contents

iii

Preface

This discussion of the financing of community and junior colleges was written with the hope that it might lead to the development of better ways of supporting the public systems run by the various states and to more financial health for private junior colleges around the country. In addition, the approach used may be helpful to those interested in other problems of public finance.

Briefly, I have attempted to put community colleges and their financing in historical perspective and have then tried to answer, to my own satisfaction, why we should be financing community colleges at all. Having done so, I developed a set of criteria that could reasonably be used to judge the pluses and minuses of any proposed financing system and discussed nine possible finance models (all but one of which is currently used in the United States) in the light of these criteria. All have some positive features, some clearly have more desirable features than do others, and none is even close to being ideal. Because of its importance and controversiality, the question of tuition is discussed separately.

Unfortunately, much current thinking about community colleges tends to be hortatory and evangelistic; it has been my intention to reject such an approach. There is little agreement, within or outside the field, as to the definition of community colleges. The American Association of Community and Junior Colleges, for example, allows each state to specify which of its institutions it wishes to be considered in this category. In the process, a few institutions are included that are rather different from the majority, and a number are excluded that would appear to the disinterested observer to qualify clearly for inclusion. This lack of agreement on what community colleges are is probably both a cause and an effect of the lack of agreement on their goals.

Economists have a good deal to tell us about the value of

education in general, but what they have to say about post-secondary education below the baccalaureate level is less than useful to us. Viewed uncritically, their results seem to indicate that the economic value of the kind of education received in community colleges is very low, and that the costs in many cases may be greater than the benefits. A critical examination of the data and results shows that such a conclusion does not seem to be warranted, but neither is it possible to come to a more satisfying conclusion. We are left with the necessity of justifying the existence of community colleges on other than purely economic grounds by asking what educational functions are currently not performed well by other institutions, but can be performed well by a community college.

Having thus justified the existence of community colleges, we approach the financing of them by establishing a set of criteria for judging any finance scheme and proceed to the development of a number of models, grouped as market economy, planned economy, and mixed economy. Each model is explained and held up to the nine criteria. Some meet more criteria well than do others and thus judgment as to the best plan must depend upon the relative value one attaches to each criterion.

In the last chapter an attempt is made to define two new models of community college finance: one, a planned-economy model, for those who prefer a unified state system of public community colleges; the other, a mixed-economy model, for those who prefer more local control. Both meet the criteria better than do any of the planned-economy models or mixed models previously discussed, and at least as well as the best of the market-economy models. And both are almost certainly more politically acceptable in the United States at the present time than would be a pure market-economy model, which would entail dismantling the system of public community colleges.

I appreciate the willing cooperation of the American Association of Community and Junior Colleges; its president, Dr. Edmund J. Gleazer, Jr., and the chairman of its Finance Committee, Bill J. Priest. However, the conclusions of this study are my own, and do not represent the position of the Association either officially or unofficially.

I also appreciate the helpfulness of the directors of the state community college systems who took the trouble to respond promptly to my questionnaire, and of Dr. Abdul Khan of the National Committee on the Financing of Postsecondary Education, who obtained for me unpublished data from the National Center for Educational Statistics.

I gratefully acknowledge the assistance of John G. Augenblick, who was particularly helpful on chapter one. Finally, I appreciate the interest of Dr. Earl Cheit, who made this study possible through a grant from the Ford Foundation.

WALTER I. GARMS

Rochester, N.Y.
May 1976

CHAPTER I

The Development of Community Colleges in the United States

THOUGH there was little in the early development of higher education in the United States to suggest their eventual development, the roots of the community college movement came, as seems befitting, from both higher and lower education. Michael Brick wrote that the American college was "shaped at first by an aristocratic establishment to meet its own ends, and later by competing denominations for whom piety and intellect were one and the same. The college was not a popular institution and had very little effect on the majority of Americans."[1] A second era of college establishment occurred with the replacement of a colonial government by a federation of states. Colleges were founded so that revenues generated from student and institutional expenditures would fall into the hands of local merchants rather than those of some neighboring state. Religious sects also developed colleges designed to train the leaders of their persuasion. This was the tradition and the community college as we know it today was not part of it.

An interesting aspect of this force of tradition is revealed by a study of the determinants of public expenditure per capita for higher education by states in years ranging from 1953–54 to 1967–68.[2] A number of determinants were tested—personal income per capita, percentage of population of college age, average years of education of the adult population, taxation as a percent of income, ratio of state to local taxes, and elasticity of yield of state taxes—and, as might be expected, personal income per capita and taxation as a percent of income were found to be important determinants. But of equal or greater importance was density of population of a state in the year 1860, a year chosen as the variable to measure the effect of tradition because the beginning of substantial public support to higher education was the passage of the Morrill (or Land Grant) Act in 1862. In the states that were sufficiently densely populated, private

1

colleges were established before the government started putting large amounts of federal money into education. Where private schools were established early, the development of public systems of higher education was later and slower than in states where higher education began to grow only with the beginning of public support.

Higher Education Antecedents of the Community College

The first important antecedent of the community college in higher education was probably the establishment of the normal school, following an example set by Horace Mann in 1839. Normal schools were, typically, the equivalent of the first two years of post-secondary education, and they concentrated on preparing their students for a useful occupation, that of teaching, rather than on Greek, Latin, and mathematics, which were the main course offerings in the colleges of the day. But the narrowly defined interest of the normal school limited its clientele. Since they were designed to serve society, normal schools were funded in part by the state. When the demand for teachers was high, some states, such as Minnesota, would repay tuition costs to any normal school graduate who had completed two years of teaching service in the state.[3]

Despite their state funding, normal schools were essentially local in constituency, aspirations, and operation. Thus, in many ways the normal school was a precursor to the community college. However, the pressures from within an institution are always toward an upgrading of its functions, for therein lies increased prestige for the employees of the institution. Nowhere can this phenomenon be seen better than in the evolution of the normal schools. All over the United States, the normal school became a teacher's college, then a state teacher's college, then a state college, and finally a state university— Illinois State University shows its antecedents by being located in Normal, Illinois.

A second important development in higher education was the recognition that even in four-year colleges education could be of a practical nature. The Morrill Act of 1862 "converted the proceeds from the sale of over 17 million acres of public lands into incentives to provide post-secondary educational opportunity."[4] The money went to the states for the establishment and operation of post-secondary institutions dedicated to the study of agriculture and mechanical and technical subjects. Within the 40 years after the passage of the Morrill Act, vocational and technical education had become a legitimate function of American higher education, and institutions providing that type of education were in healthy competition for students. Again, the internal pressure for upgrading arose. The practical orientation of the land grant college was eventually combined with the rigorous methodology of scientific investigation imported from Germany, leading to the expansion of many colleges into universities.

The process of upgrading continued with the suggestion that the undergraduate responsibilities of the university be limited. Late in the nineteenth century the notion of a "bisected college-university" was promoted by such men as Henry Tappan at the University of Michigan and William Folwell at the University of Minnesota. They were, however, unsuccessful at eliminating the first two years of post-secondary education from the curriculum. By 1896, William Rainey Harper, president of the University of Chicago, had successfully divided the four years of undergraduate education provided by his institution into a "junior" and "senior" college. This was effectively a compromise between the traditional American four-year college and the German tradition of rigorous preparation and highly selective enrollment. Harper took his solution one step further, however. He discussed with leaders of communities surrounding Chicago his notion that they expand their publicly sponsored programs and thus relieve his institution of the responsibility for the "junior" college. By 1901, at Harper's instigation, several independent junior colleges had been established in and around the city of Chicago. In addition he created the first public junior college as an extension of the high school program in the nearby city of Joliet. Harper did not ultimately eliminate the first two years of post-secondary education from the University of Chicago, but the idea conceived in Joliet was the direct forebear of the public two-year community college.

Lower Education Antecedents of the Community College

The community college movement also has its roots in American elementary and secondary education. American elementary education had its start in the New England colonies—two schools had been established by 1635. In 1642 the General Court in Massachusetts decreed that "ye chosen men" should have the power to punish by fines all parents and masters who were neglectful in "training up their children." This law established control over the parents but not over the operation of the schools. Five years later, the Massachusetts Law of 1647 required every town of 50 or more families to appoint a teacher; every town of 100 or more families was also required to appoint a schoolmaster to give instruction in Latin grammar to prepare boys for college. With the passage of this law the "New England pattern" had been established.

> The New England pattern consisted of four principles: the state could require children to be educated; the state could require towns to establish schools; the civil government could supervise and control schools by direct management in the hands of public officials; and public funds could be used for the support of public schools.[5]

In the southern colonies administration of the schools became the responsibility of parish and county officials. In the middle colonies, public authority was early used to promote education, but private control was dominant. Nonetheless, in the 1770s, when both the middle and southern colonies drew up their constitutions, the principle of public support and management of education were explicitly stated. Indeed, the middle and southern colonies took strong constitutional positions on education earlier than did the New England colonies, in spite of the leadership shown by the Puritans and their immediate heirs.[6]

Thus, by the beginning of the nineteenth century, public elementary schools were widely available, although most parents who could afford it preferred to send their children to private schools. By the middle of the nineteenth century laws requiring school attendance for at least six years had been passed in most of the states, and the public elementary schools rapidly overtook the private schools in enrollment, and began to approach them in prestige. In the middlewestern and western states, where there had been little population in the early days, few private elementary schools were ever established and public schools were the norm from the start.

While an elementary education was generally recognized as the birthright of all by the mid 1800s, few children received a high school education. Those few who did, received it in the private academies. But between 1850 and 1900 the number of public high schools grew rapidly while the private academies dwindled and disappeared. By the second decade of the twentieth century public high schools were accessible to most students, and many states had extended the age limit of their compulsory education laws to include children under the age of 16 or, in some states, 18.

During the first years of the twentieth century, a number of educators advocated the "6-4-4 plan," which conceived of public education as a 14-year venture, with six years of elementary school, four years of junior high school, and four years of senior high school. The two years of senior high school above the normal requirement were not intended as preparation for college, but as vocational study. This idea came along at the time William Rainey Harper was advocating the establishment of junior colleges, which would have taken in the first two years of undergraduate instruction. It was evident that both ends of the educational ladder were looking for an institution.

The Early Development of Junior Colleges

The first law providing for the establishment of junior colleges, known as the Caminetti Act, was passed in California in 1907. Fresno Junior College became the first legally sanctioned public junior college under that law in 1910. These colleges were originally intended to be extensions of the public high school, and were under the direct control of the local school board, but since then most of the junior colleges in California have been separated from the elementary and high schools and are operated by junior college districts. Nationwide, the origin of the community college in the confluence of pressures from both higher and lower education is reflected in the present governance of the community colleges. Some are still operated by local elementary and secondary school districts, others as branch campuses of the public university system, and many are independent of either higher or lower education.

There has been similar confusion and ambiguity in the curriculum of the community colleges. The public community college originally adhered to Harper's model, providing primarily transfer rather than terminal education. In 1917 only 17.5 percent of all programs offered in public junior colleges were terminal, but by 1921 the proportion had grown to 28 percent.[7] The shift has continued to the present time, but has been the subject of sharp controversy. It is interesting that this movement was in the opposite direction, away from the more usual one of "institutional upgrading." The reasons probably have to do with the fact that the community colleges have been more firmly under the control of the local community than were the normal schools, and certainly more than the university. The university used the junior college as a filtering device, placing all burdens on the junior college without similarly sharing in the costs incurred. The community, however, benefitted from the program whether or not the graduate of its junior college transferred to the university. As a matter of fact, it benefitted more if the college's students took

terminal courses and stayed in the community than if they transferred and did not return to the community after graduation from the
university.

Since that beginning in the early 1900s, the growth of the community colleges has been phenomenal. By 1921-22 there were 207 junior
colleges in existence, of which 69 were public. These public institutions enrolled almost half of the 16,000 students attending two-year
colleges at the time. The Depression apparently served as a catalyst to
the growth of the two-year institution, for by 1938-39 there were 575
junior colleges, of which the 258 public colleges enrolled over 70
percent of the total population served. In 1957-58, of the 667 junior
colleges, 391 were public, and enrolled almost 90 percent of the
junior college population.[8] As of October 1971, there were 2.5 million
students enrolled in 934 junior colleges. Of these, 2.4 million (96
percent) were enrolled in the 697 public community colleges,[9]
statistics that make clear the difference in size between the public
and private schools: in 1971 the average public two-year college had
3,443 students; the average private junior college had only 422
students. The largest of the public community colleges, Dade County
in Florida, had over 25,000 students.

Despite the phenomenal growth of community colleges, there is no
substantial agreement on what the community college is or what its
goals should be, nor has there ever been. The attempts to define the
institution have often ended up with statements of confusing and
meaningless generalities. In 1925 the American Association of Junior
Colleges provided a definition of the institution it represented.
Although it was an institution offering two years of work comparable
to the first two years at college, it was also "likely to develop a
different type of curriculum suited to the larger and ever changing
civic, social, religious, and vocational needs of the entire community
in which [it] is located. It is understood that in this case also the work
offered shall be on a level appropriate for high school graduates." In
1930 the definition was refined: "A fully organized junior college
aims to meet the needs of a community in which it is located,
including preparation for institutions of higher education, liberal arts
education for those who are not going beyond graduation from the
junior college, vocational training for particular occupations usually
designated as semi-professional vocations, and short courses for
adults with special interests."[10]

The debate over the role of the community college persisted even
among its most notable chroniclers. Koos, in 1925, viewed the junior
college as the last stage of secondary education.[11] Eells, in 1931, took
the position that the junior college was properly a segment of higher
education, to be distinguished from secondary education.[12] In 1940

Seashore spoke of junior colleges as providing a transition between high school and college.[13]

Bogue, in 1950, said, "It has been stated previously that the community college is not an institution. It is a movement. One of the difficulties in understanding what the community college is stems from confusion in identifying the different forms it is taking."[14] He went on to suggest that it should be an autonomous institution, serving a function independent of both high school and college. This view was essentially reiterated by Medsker in 1960 when he described the junior college as serving social needs that neither high school nor college could serve.[15]

By 1962 the institution, as viewed by Fields, was democratic, comprehensive, community centered, dedicated to life-long education, and adaptable.[16] The community college was to be accessible by all; it was supposed to meet the needs of all abilities, aptitudes, and interests, while serving the individual, the community, and society in general. Gleazer, in 1968, described the major task of the community college as the provision "of those learning experiences commonly needed as the level of educational effort in each community rises two years beyond the high school."[17] Rather than articulating the unique mission of the institution and providing a rationale for its support and operation, the goals of the community college had become all-encompassing, and thus meaningless.

Higher Education Antecedents of Community College Finance

Just as the governance and curricula of the community college have developed partly from higher education and partly from elementary and secondary education, its financing has elements of the financing of both levels. The colonial college was neither a public nor a private institution. As Jencks and Riesman point out, the colonial college . . . was seen as a public trust,

> subject to state regulation. Chartered by the state, its board of trustees often included public officials ex officio. On a year to year basis the colonial college was expected to balance its books without tax assistance, but when it needed a new building or had other "special expenses," it often appealed successfully for legislative help.[18]

Mushkin and McLoone cite Yale as an example to describe the role of finance in establishing relationships between institutions and the state. Controversy had raged over the control of Yale for a number of years prior to 1755 when the colonial assembly became dissatisfied with the management of the college and stopped its regular appropriation of public funds. The assembly debated for almost a decade whether to declare itself the true founder of the college, although control of the institution did not change. In 1792, when Yale required financial assistance, a reorganization was agreed upon which added eight state officals, including the governor, to the corporation.[19]

In general, however, the financing of higher education prior to the Civil War was a minor problem. A U.S. Supreme Court decision in an 1819 case between Dartmouth College and the state of New Hampshire affirmed the corporate independence of that institution against the efforts of a state to assume control.* This decision encouraged the private organization and control of higher education, although many states, not wishing to publicly fund institutions over which they had little control, either removed what meager support had been given to private institutions or founded new publicly controlled institutions. Of the approximately 200 institutions of higher education founded between 1790 and 1860, over 50 were founded as public institutions or became public prior to the start of the Civil War.[20] The Morrill Act of 1862 enabled the states to expand their interests rapidly in providing and controlling education, and efforts to later refund the Morrill Act met with hostility from the presidents of noted private colleges and universities whose institutions would not benefit.

After World War II the federal government massively expanded its interest in higher education with the passage of the G.I. Bill. In 1945, expenditures under this bill were $2.8-billion, which supported over one million students.[21] Direct aid to students on that scale, with no eligibility requirement beyond acceptance into a certified program, stimulated the proliferation of higher educational opportunities. In addition, increasing aid for research after the war rejuvenated the private sector of higher education, which was able to compete both for students, whose tuition would be paid for by the federal

---

*The Dartmouth College case was an important one not only in higher education, but also in the evolution of the laws which made the corporation so important in the development of our society. Dartmouth College, founded with a private endowment, was chartered as an eleemosynary institution by the state of New Hampshire, which then gave it some state money. When a disagreement arose in 1816 between the college's trustees and its president, the state stepped in and attempted to amend the charter to make the college a state institution. In 1819 the U.S. Supreme Court ruled that the state could not unilaterally amend such a charter, once granted. This gave not only colleges, but corporations in general, immunity from capricious revision of their basic character by the state. A thorough exploration of the case is in Francis N. Stotes, *Private Interest & Public Gain: The Dartmouth College Case, 1819*, Amherst: University of Massachusetts Press, 1972.

government, and for aid in support of scientific programs. The impact of this massive federal funding was to generate increased demand for higher education. Even after 1952, when most veterans had completed their education under provisions of the G.I. Bill, the demand for higher education was sustained.

For the next 15 years or so institutions of higher education grew faster than they ever had before. Facilities were added and graduate programs expanded while undergraduate enrollment doubled. Costs rose rapidly during this period, too. Inflation and the growing demand for more service, for graduate access, for innovative programs, and for higher quality strained the budgets of many institutions. While the federal government rapidly expanded its funding of higher education through the late 1950s and early 1960s, since 1967 the increases in federal support have been less than the increases in the price level.[22] Many institutions were vulnerable to a loss of income and, despite increased tuition charges, managerial reorganization, and consolidation, the "new depression in higher education," as described by Cheit, has seen many institutions operate with deficit budgets while others have been forced to terminate operation.

In recent years, the most important issues in the financing of higher education have been the following.

Private versus public education. Even in the beginning, private higher education received some government aid. Most federal aid has gone evenhandedly to private (nonsectarian) and public institutions. But, except in a few states in the Northeast, there has been little or no institutional aid to private education from state or local governments. In a few states where there were private institutions serving large numbers of students from within the state, there has been some state aid. In Pennsylvania there has been a unique partnership, with some private institutions receiving substantial state aid and becoming quasi-public through the addition of public members to their governing boards. In New York, the state has provided a system of grants to private institutions in the form of a set number of dollars for each degree granted. But nationwide, state and local money went overwhelmingly to public institutions during the period of tremendous expansion of the 1950s and 1960s, and the result has been a much more rapid expansion of the public than of the private sector of higher education.

Efficiency versus equity. Because attendance is not compulsory above the high school level, the question of whom the colleges should educate has been important. Some have argued that it is grossly inefficient to spend large sums of public money on those students who were able barely to struggle through high school. Instead, they are in favor of an elitist education of the sort that is prevalent in most of the rest of the world. Others say that equity demands that all students who wish to get a higher education should be allowed to attend some college, providing they meet the basic entrance requirements, and that low financial ability should not be a hindrance to attendance. The arguments on this issue, and some of the proposed solutions, are summarized in a report of the Joint Economic Committee of the Congress published in 1969.[23]

Grants to individuals versus institutions. Given that there should be some public support of higher education, should the money go directly to educational institutions (either in the form of general assistance or in categorical grants), or should it go directly to subsidize students? Economists generally favor the subsidization of students, on the basis that this allows the operation of the free market system. Presumably the institutions that are most efficiently run, and those offering the most attractive programs, will prosper, while the less efficient or attractive will either change or cease to exist. Predictably, those charged with the operation of institutions of higher education have strong arguments in favor of giving the grants directly to the institutions. Rivlin and Weiss have done a good job of analyzing these arguments.[24]

High tuition versus low tuition. Tuition constitutes about 25 percent of the educational and general revenue of all institutions of higher education. It constitutes a smaller percentage of the income of the public institutions, and a much higher percentage of the revenue of the private ones. Public institutions have generally taken the position that low (or no) tuition is necessary in order to make it possible for low-income students to attend. Private institutions have been concerned about the effects of competition from low-tuition public institutions. Economists have generally favored increasing the tuition in public institutions to a percentage of revenue similar to that in private institutions, in order to enhance the operation of the market mechanism.

Lower Education Antecedents of Community College Finance

A Massachusetts law of 1647 required the establishment of schools in each town, without specifying whether these were to be public or private. But by allowing that payment of the teachers and schoolmasters was to be either by the parents and masters of the children or by the "inhabitants in general," legal provision was made for the first time for support of schools through taxes. In the first half of the nineteenth century, there

. . . existed what we might call public schools, schools under public management and open to all children regardless of class or religion. But it was assumed that those parents who were able would help defray the costs of educating their children; hence rate bills, a form of tuition charge, were in common use. Children of indigent parents attended these public schools free of charge or were sent to "pauper schools," institutions maintained wholly at public expense. The idea that a household's monetary contribution to maintaining the schools should be independent of the number of children in the household had not been accepted. This is to say that the question "Why should a poor man with no children in school pay taxes to educate the children of a rich man?" had not been satisfactorily answered.[25]

By the end of the nineteenth century the rate bill had essentially disappeared, and the public schools were tuition free, although it was still the general practice to require students or their parents to purchase all of their textbooks and other supplies. The basic problem then was the inability of some districts to provide adequate schools from the proceeds of local taxes. There was some state aid in some of the states at this time, but it was small in amount, and was often simply a fixed dollar amount per school district, regardless of the number of students in the district or the local taxable wealth. The first person to have a wide impact on thinking about this problem was Ellwood P. Cubberley. In 1906 he summarized his views of the ends of state aid as follows:

Theoretically all the children of the state are equally important and are entitled to have the same advantages; practically this can never be quite true. The duty of the state is to secure for all as high a minimum of good instruction as is possible, but not to reduce all to this minimum; to equalize the advantages to all as nearly as can be done with the resources at hand; to place a premium on those local efforts which will enable communities to rise above the legal minimum as far as possible; and to encourage communities to extend their educational energies to new and desirable undertakings.[26]

Cubberley's thinking influenced many, although for years the principal form of state aid to school districts was the flat grant: a set number of dollars per student or per classroom, regardless of local ability to raise money through property taxes. This was certainly an improvement on the fixed number of dollars per district, which ignored the number of students. If the flat grant had been large, roughly equivalent in size to the amount necessary to provide an adequate minimum education to each child, it would have achieved significant equalization, but it was usually quite small.

It was not until 1923 that a new conception came along, one which incorporated the idea of equalizing for differences in local school district ability to support education. This was contained in a report to the state of New York by George D. Strayer and Robert M. Haig.[27] They proposed that the state establish the amount of expenditure per student required for an adequate minimum educational offering, and that the state guarantee every district ability to spend this much per child by levying a set rate of property tax. If the proceeds of this tax were not sufficient to provide this minimum amount of money, the state would make up the rest. This "Strayer-Haig formula" came to be known as the "Minimum Foundation Program," and was subsequently adopted by a majority of the states. Note that the basic *educational* philosophy is still that of Cubberley: the state should guarantee that each child receives a minimum education, but any expenditure beyond that minimum amount is essentially a luxury which may be indulged in by local communities to the extent they wish, without additional state aid. The only thing the minimum foundation program does is to insure that all communities will be equally able to provide the minimum education.

At about this same time, Harlan Updegraff and Leroy A. King came up with a different way for financing the public schools, based on a different philosophy. In a report on the financing of schools in Pennsylvania, they recommended that the state, in effect, become a full partner with local districts in the financing of the schools.[28] For each district a state aid ratio would be defined which would depend on a locality's fiscal ability (in terms of assessed valuation per student). The poorer the district, the higher would be the state aid ratio. The district would then decide how much it wanted to spend, and the state would provide the proportion of the expenditure called for by the district's state aid ratio. The effect would be that of allowing all districts that decided to levy the same tax rate to raise the same amount of money per student, while allowing each district the freedom to set its own tax rate.

The philosophical position of this "percentage-equalizing" formula is somewhat unusual. Essentially, it says that education is so important that the state should guarantee access to it by all on an equal basis, rather than to just some minimum amount of it. But at the same time it says that local interest in education is so important that each school district should be allowed to decide how much of this equalized education it wishes to purchase through taxes. This philosophical position was never widely adopted, although New York did in 1962, and Rhode Island used a version of it beginning in 1967. It is interesting, however, that a widely discussed book by Coons, Clune, and Sugarman in 1970 advocated "power equalizing," which is identical in philosophy to percentage equalizing.[29] In fact, it can be shown mathematically that percentage equalizing is simply a special case of power equalizing. The latter has been a popular response to the calls for school finance reform of the 1970s, and at last count almost half of the states had some form of power equalizing as part of their school finance formulas.

The last important philosophical position on educational financing was enunciated in 1930 by Henry C. Morrison.[30] His belief was that the business of education is a primary concern of the state, and is too important to be left to the vagaries of the local school boards. Rather, the state must see to it that education is provided to all on an equitable basis, with the money for education raised by statewide taxes. Essentially, he was asking for the abolition of local school districts and for the operation of elementary and secondary education as a single state system. While this position has had important supporters, it has never been adopted by any state. (Hawaii has such a system, but not because of Morrison. It had the system as a territory, and carried it over into statehood. Hawaii's total enrollment of around 180,000 students is less than that of a number of large city school districts in the United States.)

In the 1960s the main concern of those interested in elementary and secondary school finance was the plight of the cities. These were once the fair-haired of the school districts, able to offer excellent schools at low tax rates. But an influx of poor blacks and other low-income groups, combined with the exodus of industry, had put the cities in a difficult position. The cry for reform was taken up by other districts that suffered more from low taxing ability than from high concentrations of pupils with special needs. A series of court suits culminated in the 1971 decision by the California Supreme Court in *Serrano v. Priest.*[31] The essence of this decision was that the amount of money spent on a child's education should not be a function of the wealth of the school district in which he lives. Although a similar decision, *Rodriguez v. San Antonio,* was later reversed by the U.S. Supreme Court,[32] *Serrano* and several others in other states have been upheld under state constitutions.[33] These decisions would seem to invalidate any system of state support of elementary and secondary education that was not fully equalizing, including the early flat grants, and the later minimum foundation program. It would seem to allow the full state-assumption model of Henry Morrison, the percentage-equalizing of Updegraff, or the power-equalizing of Coons, Clune, and Sugarman.

In recent years, the most important issues in the financing of elementary-secondary education have been the following.

The equity issue. This has been raised in the review of the court cases. There are at least two questions involved. One is the question of whether equity in taxation is required, in the sense that equal school tax rates will produce equal expenditures per student. The other is the question of whether equity requires equal expenditure per child (for normal children), or whether expenditures may vary according to local desire so long as equity in taxation is insured. With a few states making major changes in the direction of equity, and many others dragging their heels, it is still too soon to tell what the outcome will be.

Financing urban education. City school districts have run into the twin problems of declining taxing ability and vastly increased need for special educational programs to educate the concentrations of those whose learning has been handicapped through poverty and racial discrimination.

The revolt against continual increases in property taxes. Failures of budget and bond elections have increased manyfold in the last decade, and created crisis situations in many districts.

Whether or not money makes a difference. Since the Coleman Report[34] defenders of the status quo have insisted that "equity" is not necessary because money does not make a difference in the educational achievement of children. This is not the place to try to go into this argument in any depth, but it is sufficient to say that the jury is still out. Serious objections have been raised to the methodology of the Coleman Report.[35] Other studies have reported findings similar to those of Coleman,[36] but there have been some contrary findings also.[37]

It is interesting to speculate about how many of the important issues in higher education finance and in lower education finance are applicable to the community college. All of the issues in higher education finance appear applicable. While there is little competition between private and public community colleges (because the private ones enroll fewer than 5 percent of the students), there is still competition between the community colleges and private four-year institutions, as well as between community colleges and proprietary institutions. The question of efficiency versus equity is not as strong at the community college level as it is with the four-year colleges, because the community colleges, with their policy of admitting anyone who meets the basic requirements (typically high school graduation), have come down heavily on the side of equity. The question of grants to students or institutions is as important to the community college as it is to the four-year institution. And the question of high-versus-low tuition has been an important controversy for community colleges for many years. Most advocates of and administrators in community college systems are adamantly opposed to tuition even though the current community college tuition charges are, on the average, as high a percentage of the total cost of education as tuition charges are in four-year colleges.

Equitable funding, as defined in California's *Serrano* case, has not yet become an issue to the community colleges, but it is likely that it will be, and community colleges should become familiar with the decision and possible solutions to the problems it raises: The problems of financing urban community college education are similar to those of urban public schools, for many of these colleges were established specifically to provide access to college for the inner-city student. The revolt against the property tax has been an issue with those community colleges supported partially by local property taxes. Since some community colleges are not so supported (whereas all school districts receive some of their money from property taxes), the problem is not as acute at the community college level as it is with elementary and secondary education. It also seems likely that the diversity of the community college programs will mute the question of whether money makes a difference, as it has done with higher education generally.

Thus, it appears that community colleges may be afflicted by most of the major problems in financing both higher and lower education. This certainly complicates the problems of community college finance, and makes it all the more important that a coherent conceptual framework be set up for judging methods of financing our community colleges.

The Background and Present Status of Community College Finance

Given that community colleges have origins in both higher and lower education, it is not surprising that their financing has elements of the financing of both. Actually, the financing of community colleges may have more diversity than exists in either the level below it or that above it.

The first public community colleges were clearly extensions of a local public school system, and were financed in exactly the same way as the school system. In California, the state with the most extensive community college system, that pattern persists to the present. The college is financed through a combination of local taxes and state aid, based on a minimum foundation program approach with no tuition. Other states have developed community colleges in other ways, and this has resulted in a bewildering variety of arrangements for financing them. Nevertheless, it is possible to categorize these methods, and this is done in chapters three and four where models of community college finance are discussed. However, here we can indicate in a general way the sources of money for the operation of the community colleges of the United States, and contrast that with the sources for the other institutions of post-secondary education.

As part of the research that led to this book, the sources of public community college income in 36 states and Puerto Rico, which contain 96 percent of the nation's community college students, were studied. The data are on income in 1971-72 from sources characterized as federal, state, or local, tuition fees, and other. Information was obtained on both current operating income and income for capital outlay and debt service.

Current Operating Income

There are at least two ways to look at the patterns of support for community colleges; each gives a somewhat different picture. First, one could look at an aggregation of all community colleges, converting the total number of dollars from each source into a percent of all revenue. (This is done on Table I, page 17.) Alternatively, one could look at the states individually, calculating percentages for each state and then averaging them. (See Table IV, page 19.)

Table II (page 17) makes a comparison between the sources of revenue for two-year institutions and for other institutions of higher education which reveals several things. First, the public two-year college is the only sector of higher education that receives a significant percentage of its income from local sources. Second, the public two-year colleges receive a considerably smaller percentage of their current operating income from the federal government than do public universities and four-year colleges. This percentage is, in fact, inflated since the table excludes programs such as sponsored research and major public services that receive substantial federal support at public universities and four-year colleges and very little support at public two-year colleges. Finally, it is worth noting that tuition, as a percent of income, is comparable among all public institutions, being only slightly lower at two-year colleges. This comparison is, however, distorted by the inclusion of California in

TABLE I:

Community College Revenue from Various Sources as Percent of Total for 36 States and Puerto Rico

Source	Revenue (in millions of dollars)	Percent of Total
Federal	113.4	5.2
State	955.3	44.0
Local	722.1	33.2
Tuition and Fees	306.6	14.1
Other (Including Chargebacks)	76.8	3.5
Total	2,174.2	100.0

TABLE II:

Percent of Instruction-Related Income to Institutions of Higher Education from Various Sources, 1971-72

Source*	All Institutions	Universities		Other Four-year Colleges		Two-year Colleges	
		Public	Private	Public	Private	Public	Private
Federal	10.3	10.4	11.7	13.2	7.0	8.4	8.0
State	38.6	56.3	3.8	59.5	2.3	44.3	2.0
Local	5.3	0.4	1.4	4.5	0.2	30.9	1.2
Tuition	30.0	19.5	45.9	18.5	63.1	14.3	66.5
Other	15.8	13.4	37.2	4.3	27.4	2.1	22.3

*"Instruction-related income" excludes sponsored research, recovery of indirect costs, major public service programs (mainly federally funded research and development centers and hospitals), and income from auxiliary enterprises.
  —Federal, state, and local income includes governmental appropriations, income from other (non-research) sponsored programs, and income for student aid.
  —Tuition includes fees.
  —Other includes endowment income, private gifts, other separately budgeted research (not federal, state, or local), nongovernmental sponsored programs, sales and services of educational departments, organized activities related to educational departments, other sources of educational and general revenue, private gifts and grants for student aid, endowment income for student aid, and other student aid grants.
Source: Financial Statistics of Institutions of Higher Education: Current Funds, Revenues, and Expenditures, 1971-72 (Washington, D.C.: National Center for Educational Statistics, U.S. Office of Education, 1974).

the sample. California is atypical in being the state with the most highly developed community college system and the only state in which tuition is not charged. Table III (page 19) reveals what the data would be if California were removed from the sample and treated separately.

While the community college student in California pays no tuition, his counterpart in any of the other states pays a tuition that is about 20 percent of his school's instruction costs. This is about the same average percentage of instruction costs as is paid by the student at a public university or four-year college. The only reasonable conclusion is that the cry for low or no tuition at community colleges has not, in most states, been heeded. If the absolute cost of tuition is lower in community colleges than it is in the other institutions of higher education, it is because instruction costs are lower, not because the student bears a smaller proportional burden of the cost.

Looking at the current situation from the second point of view (Table IV, page 19) requires that the percent of current income from each source be calculated for each state and then averaged over all the states. In one sense this is inappropriate, since states that spend less than $10-million a year on community colleges are combined with states spending over $100-million a year (California community colleges had an operating income of $612-million in 1971-72). If the state is viewed as the decision-making unit, however, this method of analysis is appropriate.

One advantage of doing the analysis this second way is that it makes possible a comparison over time. The percentage of income from each source for each state was studied by Arney in 1967-68. His data make possible a comparison over a period of four years for the 33 states in which data were collected for both studies. It is possible to see some trends in the direction in which patterns of support are moving; that comparison is made in Table V (page 20). The rather surprising result is that there have been substantial shifts in the pattern of support in a number of states, but their direction has not been uniform. In fact, Table V reveals a generally stable situation over a period during which costs were rising rapidly. The largest trend in the mean (if one can call a difference of three percentage points a trend) is the percentage reduction of income from local sources—from 22 percent to 19 percent.

The apparent stability indicated by Table V would not be apparent to an observer who looked at the finance pattern in a particular state. As the table shows, Arkansas, Colorado, Florida, Maryland, New Mexico, North Dakota, Tennessee, and Wyoming have assumed a substantially greater share of the current expense of operating the community colleges. In Arizona, Connecticut, Iowa, Kentucky, Mas-

TABLE III:

Percent of Community College Revenue from Various Sources Treating California Separately

Source	Percent of Total	
	35 States and Puerto Rico	**California Only**
Federal	4.5	7
State	48.2	33
Local	23.5	58
Tuition	19.6	0
Other	4.2	2

TABLE IV:

Mean, Maximum, and Minimum Percentages of Current Operating Income for Community Colleges from Various Sources

Source	Percentages				
	Mean	Maximum	(State)	Minimum	(State)
Federal	5.1	19	(Mississippi)	0	(Several)
State	53.7	90	(Puerto Rico)	15	(Kansas)
		79	(Washington)		
Local	17.8	58	(California)	0	(12 States)
Tuition	19.8	34	(Kansas)	0	(California)
Other	3.4	12	(Kentucky)	0	(Several)

TABLE V:

Percent of Income for Public Community Colleges from Various Sources, 1971-72 and 1967-1968*

State	Federal		State		Local		Tuition		Other	
	71-72	67-68	71-72	67-68	71-72	67-68	71-72	67-68	71-72	67-68
Ala.		21		59		0		18		2
Alaska	0		75		0		25		0	
Ariz.	4	3	36	47	48	43	4	1	7	6
Ark.	13	10	47	32	15	31	22	25	3	2
Calif.	7	3	33	32	58	60	0	0	2	5
Colo.	5	2	63	40	12	31	19	15	1	12
Conn.	6	1	68	79	0	0	26	20	0	0
Del.		0		100		0		0		0
Fla.	6	5	70	59	0	11	22	24	3	1
Ga.	0	4	71	69	0	0	26	25	3	2
Ha.		23		75		0		2		0
Ida.		2		40		27		24		6
Ill.	2	2	36	31	43	47	17	12	2	8
Iowa	16	12	44	55	14	17	24	14	2	2
Kans.	1	5	15	17	39	40	34	14	10	24
Ky.	6	2	70	98	0	0	12	0	12	0
La.		24		59		0		8		9
Md.	6	6	41	21	30	47	24	25	0	1
Mass.	12	4	60	71	0	0	28	25	0	0
Mich.	3	2	40	36	26	26	26	29	5	7
Minn.		2		71		0		27		0
Miss.	19	11	43	39	23	35	15	11	0	4
Mo.	8	5	27	31	32	37	23	17	10	10
Mont.	6	4	45	59	17	20	25	17	6	0
Neb.		0		26		35		33		6
Nev.		0		4		0		34		62
N.J.	2	0	42	50	29	25	26	25	1	0

TABLE V: (Cont.)

Percent of Income for Public Community Colleges from Various Sources, 1971-72 and 1967-1968*

State	Federal		State		Local		Tuition		Other	
	71-72	67-68	71-72	67-68	71-72	67-68	71-72	67-68	71-72	67-68
N.M.	7	11	39	0	22	33	30	51	3	5
N.Y.	2	2	36	32	35	38	20	21	8	7
N.C.	8	2	75	79	11	11	7	8	0	0
N.D.	1	8	54	42	10	20	31	29	3	1
Ohio	1	2	32	36	46	25	20	30	2	7
Okla.	0	0	60	59	3	4	26	32	11	5
Ore.	3	7	49	48	27	22	22	23	0	0
Penn.	0	7	33	31	33	31	33	31	0	0
R.I.	0	1	70	63	0	0	23	18	7	18
S.C.	11		69		10		11		0	
Tenn.	7	15	75	62	0	0	14	13	4	10
Texas	3	0	57	51	20	30	17	19	4	0
Utah	8	8	66	67	0	0	22	24	4	1
Va.	11	10	71	79	0	0	17	11	1	0
Wash.	6	11	79	76	0	0	11	13	4	0
Wisc.	4		33		57		6		0	
Wyo.	3	4	45	31	39	43	13	17	0	5
P.R.	6		90		0		4		0	
Mean of those reported for both years:										
	6	5	51	49	19	22	20	20	4	5

*A blank space in a column indicates that no data was collected for that state for that year. (Columns may not add up to 100 due to rounding.)

Source: Data are for public community colleges as defined by each reporting state. Data for 1971-72 are from answers to questionnaires sent from the American Association of Community and Junior Colleges to state community college coordinators in 1973. Data for 1967-68 are from Lawrence H. Arney, State Patterns of Financial Support for Community Colleges (Gainesville: Institute of Higher Education, University of Florida, 1970).

sachusetts, Montana, New Jersey, and Virginia, however, a shift away from the state as a source of funding has occurred. The pattern is somewhat different with the local share. In Ohio the local contribution has increased substantially while it has decreased substantially in Arkansas, Colorado, Maryland, Mississippi, New Mexico, North Dakota, and Texas.

The percent of income from tuition and fees has increased substantially in Iowa, Kansas, and Kentucky, while it has decreased in New Mexico and Ohio. In most states tuition, as a percent of current income, has stayed relatively the same. It appears, then, that the major forces active during this time period have been accommodations to the changing financial ability and willingness of state and locality, rather than an attempt to reduce the tuition burden to the student. Tuition income, as a percent of current income, has remained constant. The fact is, however, that with educational costs rising more quickly than personal income, the absolute burden on the student has increased.

Capital Outlay and Debt Service

Information about revenue sources for capital outlay and debt service was also requested as part of the study. Usable information was received from 31 states. The results for the public community colleges in these states are given in Table VI (page 19). It is clear that capital improvements are financed almost exclusively by the state and/or locality with state contributions far outweighing local contributions. In a number of states 90 percent or more of the money for capital purposes comes from a single source: from the state in Alaska, Connecticut, Florida, Massachusetts, Ohio, Rhode Island, and Puerto Rico; from local sources in Kansas, Missouri, New Mexico, North Dakota, and South Carolina; in Kentucky and Washington, it comes from tuition and fees. Other states usually employ some form of state aid to help localities with capital outlay and debt service expense. Maryland, New York, and Pennsylvania, for example, share capital expenditures equally between state and locality. California uses an equalized form of aid in which those community college districts below a certain property wealth per pupil are eligible for state assistance, with the poorest districts receiving the largest amounts.

Due to a lack of sufficient data it is impossible to analyze changing patterns in the funding of capital expense. It has been argued that a state is more favorable toward providing capital funds when community colleges are state controlled, and the growing tendency

TABLE VI:

Capital Outlay and Debt Service Revenue for Public Community Colleges from Various Sources for 31 States

Source	Revenue (in millions of dollars)	Percent of Total
Federal	21.1	3.8
State	393.5	70.2
Local	123.1	22.0
Tuition	10.7	1.9
Other	11.9	2.1
Total	560.3	100.0

toward state control would, therefore, imply that states have been increasingly involved in providing funds for capital outlay. Some states have, however, required local communities to provide land or to share, in some other way, in the provision of capital expenses.

The fact that the community college has antecedents in both higher education and lower education has been of great importance to its development. In curriculum, the portion that arose from higher education emphasized transfer programs; while that which came from elementary and secondary education emphasized terminal programs. These twin threads, of transfer and terminal programs, are still controversial in community colleges today.

Just as the curriculum of the community colleges reflects their origins in both higher and lower education, so does the governance of these colleges. They are governed as extensions of public school districts, as branches of the state university system, or as independent entities. Two, or perhaps all three, of these patterns may occur in the same state.

This duality is also reflected in the financing of community colleges. Some are financed as if they were institutions of higher education, some are financed as if they were part of elementary and secondary education, and some are financed in a way that is a combination of the two. As a result, both the issues that face the financing of higher education and those that face the financing of lower education are, at least potentially, issues in the financing of community college education. This makes it very important to establish a framework for thinking about how we should finance the community colleges, which is the subject of the rest of this book.

CHAPTER II

Functions and Finances of Community Colleges

BEFORE considering how to finance community colleges, it seems proper to ask whether or not they are worth financing: is there a firm economic rationale for supporting them? Can financing a system of community colleges be justified rationally on a basis that is a combination of economic and social logic?

When we consider that post-secondary education is costly to individuals in time and money, and costly to society in subsidies that have alternative uses, it is clear that it is important to examine its costs and benefits, and to compare those costs and benefits with alternative activities that might be undertaken. Economists have developed some of the tools necessary for this kind of analysis, and they have something to say about education. Unfortunately, as in most areas of human endeavor, neither the economist nor anyone else has definitive answers.

Money is the common denominator of economics because it has no intrinsic value, but may be used to purchase a very wide variety of things that are of value. Money is used for purchases that can be thought of as either consumption or investment and education has both consumption and investment aspects. Many people actually enjoy the activities associated with acquiring an education. They also may acquire knowledge that will enrich their lives in future years, such as an appreciation for classical music, and thus enjoy a stream of consumption benefits over an extended period of time. But most people tend to think of education as an investment that will bring them monetary returns in the form of additional income over a period of years.

It is also possible for society to benefit over and above the benefits to individuals. Better educated individuals may be better citizens, enriching the lives of those around them, operating our democracy more wisely and fairly, and committing less crime. An educated person may also be able to direct the work of less-educated people, enabling them to earn more than they would if they were not so directed. All of these things are benefits that accrue to individuals other than those who invested in the education, and thus are external benefits rather than individual benefits. The existence of these external benefits has often been used as the justification for public spending on education.

Many of the benefits of education are of a non-monetary sort, and on examination many of the costs would be found to be non-monetary also. This puts the economist in a quandary, for he deals with money. Almost all consumption benefits turn out to be non-monetary and many investment benefits are also. The result of this is that economists, although they acknowledge the existence of non-monetary benefits and costs, tend to ignore them in their calculations. This means that the analysis by economists of educational costs and benefits has dwelt almost exclusively with the investment aspects of education, and within that category, with those to which a dollar value can be attached. In a society that places such a high value on the kinds of material things that can be purchased with money, the one-sidedness of this kind of analysis has not been as striking as it might have been in another society.

The Benefits and Costs of Post-Secondary Education

What *have* economists been able to tell us about the benefits and costs of education? They have been able to show us that the returns to education are substantial, but not so great as many people might believe. In 1972 a person with a college degree could expect to earn, over his lifetime, $196,902 more than a person with only a high school diploma. High school counselors have been comparing figures like this to the cost of college (say $12,000) and convincing students that a college education will return to them many times its cost. What they fail to appreciate is that money has time value: that a dollar to be received some years from now does not have the same value as a dollar in hand. There are a number of reasons for this: inflation, the fact that money may be invested at interest, the fact that one may have a use for the money now, the uncertainty of receiving the money in the future. All of these increase the value of money one has now compared with money one may receive at a later date. Economists make allowance for this with the concept of *present value*.

In computing present value, economists adopt an interest rate, which they call the discount rate. The higher the discount rate, the greater value one puts on money in hand compared with money in the future. They then calculate the present value of the sum of money to be obtained in the future by asking how much money would have to be invested now at the discount rate in order to have that sum of money at that time in the future. For example, at age 60 a person with a college education may be making $10,000 more than a person with a high school education. But to the person in high school at age 18 trying to decide whether to undertake the college education that $10,000 at a discount rate of 10 percent has a present value of only $183. That is, if one put $183 in the bank at 10 percent interest, in 42 years he would have $10,000. The closer to the present the receipt of money occurs, the greater its present value. This same person at age 18 would find that the present value of the $3,000 additional annual income he might earn at age 30 would be $956.

If we assumed that the $196,902 in additional earnings of a college graduate were earned in equal increments over his working lifetime (from 22 to 65), he would earn an additional $4,579 a year. The present value at age 18 of this stream of additional income would be $30,756. It is unlikely that the additional income would be earned in equal increments, though, and all reasonable assumptions one might make about it would lower the present value. A present value of about $20,000 is more reasonable, and this can be compared with the present value of the cost of college, which might be around $10,000. Clearly, this is a profitable undertaking, *on the average,* but whether it will be for a particular individual is a question the economist cannot answer.

Comparing the benefits in terms of present value of increased lifetime income with the costs of obtaining the education, economists have found that the return to an elementary education is highest, followed by that to a high school education, then by the return to four years of college. On the average, one could expect that an individual investment in four years of college would bring a return over the years (properly discounted) that would exceed the return on the same money invested in the stock market (even when the market is "normal"). The return on a postgraduate education is lower, *and the lowest rate of return is on one to three years of college education.*[1] For male blacks, the return to one to three years of college education may even be less than zero; that is, the benefits may be less than the costs.[2]

To the person who believes in the value of community colleges these results, if true without qualification, would be a severe blow. But there are a number of qualifications, and they are important ones. Many of them are technical, but some can be easily understood. First, in making their calculations, economists have used aggregated data, usually for the United States as a whole. They have been forced to rely on data collected by the Census Bureau, which has no separate category for community college education. Those who have had some education beyond high school but have not graduated from college are put in the category of "one to three years of college" regardless of whether they dropped out of a four-year college, received an A.A. degree from a two-year college, completed a non-degree technical program, or took a few college courses for their own enjoyment. The results that show low return to an investment in "one to three years of college" are at best meaningless, then, or at worst seriously misleading. They have been used to deny the value of community colleges, and to discourage those who are unlikely to complete four years of college (because of low income or poor academic performance) from enrolling in college.

Second, even if there were a meaningful category for "community college education" in the Census Bureau data (and the offerings of community colleges are so heterogeneous that it is doubtful that such a category would be meaningful) we would still not have the information we need, because of a second difficulty. The benefits of education are conceived of by economists as the present value of the stream of additional income that comes to the recipient of the education over his lifetime. But we cannot wait until those who are now receiving their education have completed their life's work and retired to find out how valuable that education is. So we take the earnings of people with a college education who are now 50 years old as representing what the earnings of present college students will be when they are 50 years old. In other words, we infer longitudinal data from present cross-sectional data. The problem, of course, is that people who are now 50 years old may have had a very different kind of college education than present students are receiving. In particular, people who are now 50 years old and who had "one to three years of college" will not, in most cases, have had any education in a community college, for the nationwide spread of community colleges is a recent phenomenon. Thus, again we are on very weak ground in trying to infer from the studies of economists the value of a community college education.

Third, most of the studies that have been done to date have used data aggregated across all occupations. Thus, those who became ministers, teachers, and businessmen have all been lumped under the same category if they had the same number of years of education. Yet it is unlikely that the minister, at least, will get enough monetary return to justify the costs of his education. (Why, then, does he undertake the education? Because he values highly some non-monetary returns having to do with helping his fellow humans, and this makes up for the lack of monetary income. But these non-monetary returns are not evaluated by the economists.) The returns to all kinds of people, regardless of their fields of endeavor, are averaged together, and the result is not helpful to the individual who wishes to know the chances of getting a return on his investment in education. There have been a few studies that have attempted to look at the returns to education in particular fields, but the data problems are severe, and the fields covered so far are few.

Fourth, it is clear that at present (and even more so in the past), a person who shows academic ability is more apt to receive a college education. Persons with more academic ability (as measured by "intelligence" tests) are also apt to come from more well-to-do families. Thus, the fact that college graduates earn more may be partly because they are more able, and would have earned more even if they had not had a college education. Because they come from families with a higher socioeconomic status, they may also be able to exploit family ties and friendship to get jobs that earn them more money and might even have been able to do so had they not had a college education. In other words, the return received from an investment in a college education is mixed with the return from having more ability, and the return from nepotism. No one knows the extent to which the returns are caused by education and the extent to which they are merely associated with education, and we are not apt to find out soon. There have been estimates made that the percent of the increase in income associated with education *caused* by education is anywhere from 60 percent to 90 percent; but one can have little confidence in the estimates. This factor is of particular importance in evaluating the returns to a community college education, where the students are less apt to be of high "ability" or to come from well-to-do homes. This also could help to explain the lower returns to "one to three years of college."

Fifth, the costs that are calculated, in order to arrive at an estimated rate of return, are usually based on the costs of attending a four-year college. To the extent that these are higher than the costs of attending a community college, the returns to a community college education would be underestimated.

Sixth, the non-monetary benefits and costs of getting a post-secondary education have been acknowledged, but not taken into account. As was mentioned earlier, the benefits to an individual of an investment in education as a minister are clearly sufficient to induce some individuals to bear the costs of the education, but most of the returns are non-monetary. In addition, consumption benefits tend to be ignored completely because they are non-monetary, although they may constitute an important part of the benefits in an individual's calculations.

Seventh, there is no consensus among economists about the

relative size of external benefits and private benefits of education. A major reason for this is that many of the social benefits are non-monetary, just as is the case with individual benefits. There are some economists who believe that the external benefits of higher education are substantial, and others who argue that almost all of the benefit of higher education goes to the individual who obtains it. The argument is of more than academic interest, for it is much more difficult to support an argument for government subsidization of higher education if all of the benefits of the education go to the individuals who obtain it. This belief that the external benefits of higher education are vanishingly small is an important part of the intellectual underpinning for proposals to reduce government subsidization and increase tuition at public institutions of higher education.

To summarize, the studies by economists of returns to education have indicated that, when viewed as investment, most education yields greater returns to the individual and to society than investing the same amount in the typical alternative investment, such as stocks. The rate of return generally decreases with level of education, from elementary school to graduate education. But the lowest returns appear to be those resulting from obtaining one to three years of college. The data and conceptual problems here are such that we can have little confidence in inferring from them the value of a community college education. And the studies tell us next to nothing about the value of particular programs of study within the community college. Obviously, more research in this particular area is badly needed, but it should be clear from the foregoing discussion that it will not be easy to get definitive results.

The Special Capabilities and Functions of Community Colleges

While economists can make some statements about the benefits of higher education in a general way, they have so far been able to provide us with little guidance as to the relative benefits of different types of higher education (community colleges, liberal arts colleges, universities, technical institutes, etc.), or of different educational programs within each group of institutions. This leaves us with a dilemma, for legislators and the public are increasingly wanting to know whether they are getting their money's worth out of the evermounting expenditures for education. One approach that may be helpful, and that gives some guidance in evaluating alternative financing plans, is to allege the general value of higher education, based on studies by economists and others, and then to suggest that there are certain educational functions that community colleges are best qualified or uniquely qualified to accomplish. This leads to a discussion of the mission and identity of the community colleges.

While it is fashionable in many quarters to talk of developing institutional goals, when it comes to actually doing this most people find it exasperatingly difficult. It is usually only possible to reach consensus on goals by stating them so broadly that they are almost useless as guidelines. Making goals thus usually turns out to be an exercise in frustration. But, on the other hand, the traditional institutions of higher education have been in existence a long time, and have a set of implicit goals. Most people would probably be able rather quickly to reach general consensus on what these goals are, whether or not they think these are what they should be. Similarly, the traditional institutions have a form and identity established over time, so that it is not at all difficult in most cases to identify a university or a four-year college.

Such is not the case with the community colleges. There is consensus neither on what the community colleges are nor what they should be doing. No uniform definition exists, and the American Association of Community and Junior Colleges has been forced, in its *Junior College Directory,* to accept as junior or community colleges those that the state says are such.[3] An example of the confusion is the state of Wisconsin, where the *Junior College Directory* lists 28 public junior colleges, seven of them with membership in A.A.C.J.C. But the questionnaire used as part of the study on which this book is based was returned from Wisconsin listing only three community colleges. Inspection of the *Junior College Directory* reveals that 11 of the public two-year colleges in Wisconsin are branches of the University Center System. The other 17 belong to the Vocational Technical and Adult Education System. Most of those in the latter system are called technical institutes, but three are called technical colleges, and are presumably the ones referred to in the answers to the questionnaire. It is to be presumed that the technical institutes are the equivalent of area vocational centers, which also exist in many other states. But most states have not listed them in the *Junior College Directory.* As a matter of fact, the area vocational centers are the real orphans of education. They are apparently considered to be neither higher nor lower education, and no one gathers data on them. Though they are funded substantially by the federal government, even the U.S. Office of Education does not publish data on them. Most of the data published on students in educational institutions completely ignores the rather large number in these technical institutes.

This discussion is neither for the purpose of suggesting that area vocational centers (or, for that matter, two-year branch campuses of universities) should be considered as community colleges. Rather, it is an example of the problems faced by a new concept struggling to establish for itself an identity and a mission. In a sense, one of the strengths of the community college movement is the thing that makes it hard to analyze. That is the fact that it has not been hidebound by traditional forms that can be easily categorized and counted. But this diversity has also made it difficult for the community colleges to band together as a powerful force to influence legislation, as other segments of education have been able to do.

The same problem arises when one talks about the mission of the community college. Most community college people tend to think of offering programs that can be categorized as transfer (first two years of college), terminal (vocational courses for recent high school graduates), and community service (vocational, avocational, and academic courses for those who are past the usual college age). But the community colleges are not the only ones to offer such programs. The four-year institutions obviously offer the first two undergraduate years. The high schools and the area vocational centers offer vocational courses. And both high schools and university extension programs offer adult education courses.

Many in the community colleges would argue that it is not so much that the community colleges offer something no one else offers, but that they bring together in one place, at the local community level, a number of different things that are desired by those in the local community and that can be classified as educational. A basic difficulty with this approach is that it fosters a department store approach: the community college offers anything educational that seems to be wanted by the local community and that is not otherwise being provided. There is nothing intrinsically wrong with this approach, except that it inevitably raises questions of how much of this sort of thing should be subsidized by public money. This is not a trivial question, as is reflected by the fact that many states will not subsidize community college offerings of avocational courses.

The question of how community college education should be financed is intimately tied up with our conception of the functions of the community college in our society. Milton Friedman and some other economists have argued that government funding of education is justified only to the extent that there are external benefits that do not directly benefit the student, and to the extent that there are market imperfections that inhibit optimum consumption of education.[4] They agree that one social benefit of education is that of equality of educational opportunity and resulting increased social mobility. Jerome Karabel, of the American Council on Education, argues that the community colleges, far from doing this, have merely served to preserve the existing stratified social structure while contributing to what he calls educational inflation:

> The process by which the educational system expands without narrowing relative differences between groups or changing the underlying opportunity structure may be referred to as "educational inflation". . . . Like economic inflation, educational inflation means that what used to be quite valuable (e.g., a high school diploma) is worth less than it once was. As lower socioeconomic groups attain access to a specific level of education, educational escalation is pushed one step higher. . . . The net effect of educational inflation is thus to vitiate the social impact of extending educational opportunity to a higher level.
>
> If the theory of educational inflation is correct, we would expect that the tremendous expansion of the educational system in the twentieth century has been accompanied by minimal changes in the system of social stratification. Indeed, various studies indicate that the rate of social mobility has remained fairly constant in the last half-century, as has the distribution of wealth and income.[5]

To the extent that people have expected education in general, and community colleges in particular, to help to reduce the extremes of affluence and poverty in our society (and it must be admitted that this argument is frequently used), the purported social benefits have apparently not accrued. However, it should be made clear just what it is that Karabel is talking about. He is talking about equality of status, not equality of educational opportunity. He stands clearly for a vast leveling of the range of socioeconomic statuses, of a sort that has only been accomplished (if at all) in the People's Republic of China. It is doubtful that most Americans are in favor of this much leveling. On the other hand, the general direction of political and social policy since the days of the New Deal has been in the direction of more leveling. The educational system has been thought of as a primary tool in this policy, and it is interesting that the results, up to the present, have apparently been minimal.

It can be argued that raising the standard of living for everyone is an important end in itself, and it is clear that this has been done dramatically during the last 40 years. Karabel notes this, and agrees that it may raise general levels of satisfaction, Richard Easterlin, an economist at the Wharton School of Finance, disputes this. He cites a number of studies that show, for a particular point in time, in a single country, that the better off a person is economically, the happier he is. But he points out that the relationship does not hold over time or over countries:

> The showing of both sets of data—international and historical—does *not* conform to what one would expect on the basis of the positive relation between happiness and income prevailing *within* countries. Richer countries are not typically happier than poorer ones. In the United States, the average level of happiness in 1970 was not much different from that in the late 1940's, though average income, after allowance for taxes and inflation, could buy over 60 per cent more. By and large, the evidence indicates no relation—positive or negative—between happiness and national income. Whether the people in a particular time or place are comparatively happy is seemingly independent of the average level of income. [*Emphasis in original.*]
>
> . . .
>
> Are we then trapped in a material rat-race, "hooked" on what Philip Brickman and Donald T. Campbell more euphemistically call a "hedonic treadmill"? The argument points to this uncomfortable conclusion. Each person acts on the assumption that more money will bring more happiness; and indeed, if he does get more money, and others do not (or get less), his happiness increases. But when everyone acts on this assumption and incomes generally increase, no one, on the average, feels better off. Yet each person goes on, generation after generation, unaware of the self-defeating process in which he is caught up. To the outside observer, economic growth appears to be producing an ever more affluent society, but to those involved in the process, affluence will always remain a distant, urgently sought, but never attained goal.[6]

These indictments, if they can be accepted, cast serious doubt on two of the purported external benefits of education: decreasing socioeconomic disparities, and increasing the general standard of living. If would be interesting to see whether the studies show that relative happiness of inhabitants of different nations is correlated with the degree of socioeconomic disparity in the country. If they do not, we must ask ourselves whether the criterion of happiness is an appropriate one and whether the studies have been properly done. If the answer to both of these questions is yes, we must ask whether we should waste our time pursing the goals of economic development and social leveling, and instead pursue some other goals.

However, Karabel makes it clear that he is not denying the function of the community colleges in promoting individual social mobility. Even if we accept the fact that there will continue to be substantial socioeconomic differences within the United States, it seems reasonable on the basis of equity to do what we can to increase the opportunity for social mobility. There is not much direct evidence on the extent to which community colleges increase social mobility. A study by Vincent Tinto entitled "Public Junior Colleges and the Substitution Effect in Higher Education" is interesting more for the way in which he approaches the subject than for his findings.[7] He asks the question, "To what extent does the presence of a community college in a community influence the rate of completion of a bachelor's degree by high school graduates of the community?" He did a cross-tabular analysis of over 8,000 Illinois high school graduates of different sex, ability, and social class backgrounds, some from areas with community colleges and some from areas with no community college and found that:

> For both males and females in Illinois, it was clear that individuals from communities without a local college were more likely to complete a four-year college degree upon entering college than were similar persons from communities with a local public junior college. Recalling that the calculations ignored the direct effect of one's social class upon predicted rates of completion, it was noteworthy that while there was little difference in rates of degree completion among college-entrants of differing social classes in communities without a local college, social status and predicted completion rates were directly related among college-entrants from communities with a local public junior college.
>
> Differences in predicted rates of college completion between comparable college-entrants living in communities with and without a local public junior college were inversely related to father's occupational level and were largest for lower status persons in the higher ability quarters. In other words, the degree to which the local public junior college accessibility was associated with lower rates of four-year college completion was greatest for those college-entrants for whom these institutions are supposedly designed to improve chances for college completion.[8]

Of course, Tinto has only used completion of a four-year college as one indication of the extent to which community colleges contribute to social mobility, and his study can be subjected to the same kind of analysis and criticism that were leveled at the studies of the economists. What is important is that, although many in the community college field have been confining themselves to hortatory and normative declarations, a few people in other fields have been beginning to develop research findings based on reasonable research design. As more become interested, their designs and their data will improve. But they will look for those things that interest them most, and they may not be the things that interest the community college people most. It would be unfortunate if, because of this, many findings were harmful to the community college movement without at least an attempt to come out with some solidly based research on the questions that are vital to those in the community colleges.

In spite of the difficulty of defining the identity of the community college or its mission, one can conceive of three functions that characterize most of the institutions people think of as community colleges, and that can reasonably be used as justifications for the existence of the institutions. These three special functions, or how well a community college serves them, will later be cited as three of the nine criteria established in this book to evaluate the financing plans discussed in chapters three and four.

The first special function is that community colleges provide access to post-secondary education for those who find access to traditional institutions difficult or impossible, and thus community colleges encourage social mobility. There are several groups that can be put into this category, and the community colleges have attempted through various means to serve all of them. These groups are listed below.

Those who find access through traditional institutions difficult because of the cost involved. This does not include only the truly poor. As the cost of a college education has increased, the children of the middle class have found college a much greater problem. At the same time, student aid often is targeted to the poor, leaving the middle-class student in a bind at both ends. Community colleges have served this group through policies of low tuition and a proximity that allows the student to live at home.

Those whose academic ability and performance are too poor to allow them access to four-year institutions using selective admissions policies. Community colleges have served these students through their open-door policy that guarantees admission to any high school graduate (and to some who did not graduate).

Those who live too far from a four-year institution. This is, of course, closely tied to the financial problem, for most students with sufficient money would be willing to attend a four-year institution some distance away. But there are some who would find this impossible regardless of the money involved: the person with a good job in the community, the mother with small children, and others. Community colleges serve this group by establishing colleges in communities that do not have four-year institutions.

Those who are beyond the usual college age. The four-year institutions tend to think in terms of full-time students who are in their late teens and early twenties. They typically have little or no concern with those who are older, in spite of the fact that these older persons may have a much better idea what they want out of education and are thus better motivated to learn. Community colleges serve this group by providing courses that are of interest to them, and by offering courses at times other than the normal working hours. (See Appendix One.)

The second function is that community colleges provide courses and programs that are not provided, or are insufficiently provided, by the four-year institutions: vocational courses, avocational courses, short-term programs, non-degree programs, and other similar offerings.

The third function served by community colleges is that they have a commitment to offer those programs that are most needed in the local community, as determined by that community, A four-year institution likes to think of itself as having a statewide, regional, or even national appeal. The special needs of the community in which it is located are of little concern to such a college. Conversely, the very name "community college" emphasizes its commitment to meeting local needs.

It is on the basis of these special capabilities that community colleges should be able to justify their separate existence. Prominent in the list of criteria for judging financing programs for community colleges should be the extent to which the program enhances or impedes the college in meeting these special capabilities.

Criteria for Judging Financing Plans for Community Colleges

Any discussion of alternative ways of achieving a goal implies criteria by which to judge the relative value of the alternatives. The criteria that will be used for judging the various finance models discussed in this book are given below. Those who disagree with the criteria may subsitute others (see Appendix Two) or examine the models in the light of their own criteria. It should be noted that the criteria may tend to conflict, so that maximizing the extent to which one criterion is met may reduce the extent to which another is met. The first three criteria concern how well a community college finance plan helps these institutions meet the special functions they are established to serve. Rephrased as criteria for judging finance plans, these three are:

1. *The finance program should enhance, rather than impede, the ability of the community college to serve those who find access to traditional institutions difficult.*

2. *It should enhance, rather than impede, the ability of the community colleges to provide courses and programs not provided, or provided insufficiently, by the four-year institutions.*

3. *It should enhance, not impede, the ability of the community college to respond to the particular needs of the community it serves.*

The others are discussed more fully below.

4. *The finance program should help to preserve the health and independence of the private sector of higher education, both two-year and four-year.*

Private higher education was established in the United States before public higher education, and has long been an important part of the higher education enterprise. It was only during the 1950s that enrollment in public higher education exceeded that in private higher education. These private institutions operate at a much lower cost to the taxpayers than do public institutions, and to force them out of existence and build public institutions to replace them would be an enormous public expense. This additional expense would decrease the relative amount of money per student that present public institutions have available. Thus, it is in the financial interest of the public sector to see to it that the private sector remains viable.

In addition, the private institutions, because of their independence, have been able to differentiate themselves and to offer special programs and services that the public institutions have not. It is in the public interest to see that this is allowed to continue because it not only meets the needs of special students, but often points the way for innovation in the public sector.

5. *The finance program should help to keep the expansion of the community colleges within the bounds of public willingness to support them, and should take into account the financial health of*

state and local governments and the competing demands upon them for money.

The total amount of money allocated to community colleges by state and local governments is, of course, determined through the political process. This is as it should be, because in this way the judgments of elected representatives are brought to bear on questions of the absolute level of funding, and of the relative emphasis to be given to community college education and to all of the other needs competing for the public purse. But each operation that is supported by public money tends to see its needs as most urgent, and to ignore or downgrade the needs of other operations. This is particularly true of those operations, like community colleges, that in many states are semi-independent operations, and have a separate budget rather than bargaining for their share of a consolidated state or municipal budget. Open-ended funding patterns that allow institutions to expand without limit can enhance the college's feeling of independence while making legislatures and the public feel that the colleges have a pipeline to the treasury with no valve on it.

6. *The finance program should help to prevent wasteful duplication among institutions, and among the levels of education: secondary schools, community colleges, area vocational schools, liberal arts colleges, universities, specialized technical schools.*

Because education is so massively supported by public funds, the public is rightly concerned that the various institutions it supports do not wastefully duplicate expensive programs and facilities. In states where there is substantial public support of private institutions, there is even concern about wasteful duplication that might be engaged in by the private sector. In New York, for example, the state board of regents from 1970 to 1973 put a moratorium on new doctoral programs that applied to all institutions in the state, public and private. While the arrangements to avoid duplication are more in the management than the finance area, the form of the finance program can affect such duplication positively or negatively. This criterion might be thought of as saying that the finance program should promote *inter*-institutional efficiency.

7. *The finance program should encourage the various colleges to operate their own programs efficiently.*

One of the serious problems with education, both public and private nonprofit, is that there is no simple goal akin to that of making a profit. Thus there are not the strong incentives to operate efficiently that there are in private business. However, a good finance program can help to provide such incentives, and a poor one can lessen them. This criterion could be thought of as *intra*-institutional efficiency.

8. *The finance program should provide equity to the students of the colleges.*

Chapter one outlined the basis of the suits that have been filed in more than half of the states to challenge the method of financing the public elementary and secondary schools. In the best known of these, *Serrano* v. *Priest,* the California Supreme Court found the method of financing the public schools in the state to be unconstitutional under both federal and state constitutions.[9] Stripped of its legal complexities, the decision concerns the combination of local taxes and state aid that finances public schools in California. While property-poor school districts receive more state money per student than do property-rich districts, the difference is not enough to offset the difference in ability to raise money through local taxes. Thus, some school districts can support their schools handsomely at a low property tax rate, but others must levy a much higher tax rate and have less per student to spend. The *Serrano* decision declared that education is a responsibility of the state, and that the amount spent on education should not depend upon the financial ability of a locality, but only upon that of the state as a whole. This decision, and similar decisions in a number of other states, have thus far dealt only with the elementary and secondary schools. But there is no reason to believe that the same reasoning cannot be successfully applied to a state's community college system, if it is partially financed by local taxes. It is significant that the method of financing the community colleges in California is almost identical in form to that used for the elementary and secondary schools. But regardless of whether or not a successful court case challenging community college financing is brought, the principle seems a reasonable one, and is included here as a criterion: the quality of the education provided at a community college should be dependent upon the wealth of the state as a whole, and not upon the wealth of the community served by the college.

9. *The finance program should provide equity to the taxpayers who support it.*

This criterion is also implied in the *Serrano* doctrine: the taxpayers of two communities should not have to make different tax effort to provide identical community college education. But in the models of community college finance that follow, it turns out that a model that meets one of these criteria does not necessarily meet the other, and so the two are stated separately.

CHAPTER III

Financing
Community Colleges:
Free Market Models

THERE is an infinite number of ways to finance community colleges, if we take into account the varying percentages of income from various sources, and the ways in which these amounts are determined. But the conceptual models for possible financing plans are limited in number; these models are discussed below, including the application of the nine criteria to each model. Each represents a financing method in a more or less "pure" form, though possibly none is suitable for adoption in that pure form. But the models can be combined in various ways, and the summary at the end of the book will attempt to show some ways this could be done to make a model that better fits the criteria. It would be foolish to prescribe a single financing model suitable for all states. Each state will have to decide for itself the best financing method to use; the situation in each is in some measure unique but the principles discussed here have general applicability.

Financing methods can be broadly categorized into three groups: market-economy models, which are discussed in this chapter, and the planned-economy models and mixed models, which are discussed in chapter four. Each group contains specific variations of these models. Only one of the models, that of power equalizing, does not currently exist in the United States.

The Free Market Economy and Education

The United States developed as, and still is predominantly, a market economy. That is, it is an economy in which entrepreneurs are free to establish businesses and produce goods and services at will, with few restrictions on them. There is no concern about duplication of effort and no central control over what is to be

41

produced and how much of it. Rather, the profit motivation operating through the market system determines these things. The "invisible hand" of the market acts to see that goods and services are produced and are available to meet the demands of the public, and it also insures that those who produce these things most efficiently prosper and those who are least efficient fail.*

Economists in the western world feel comfortable with the market economy. It is the economy toward which almost all of their theoretical training has oriented them. It is natural, then, that when they start thinking of education and how it should properly be financed, they should think in terms of the market economy. Of course, these economists admit that there are some things that should be financed, and even operated, by the government. National defense is a prime example, and the reason it must be operated by the government is that there is no feasible way to limit the benefits of national defense to those who choose to pay for it. Given the choice, no one would be willing to buy national defense on the open market, because one can get it free, since the government cannot defend others without defending each of us individually. Thus, national defense becomes a matter of compulsion for the individual, with the decision as to the amount of expenditure and what it is expended for a collective one.

A second sort of thing that is usually financed by the government, even though it is feasible to limit enjoyment of it to those who pay for it, is the kind of thing that costs so much that private enterprise might not be willing to make the investment. Highways are an example, as is the traffic control system that regulates our airways.

A third kind of government-financed expenditure is for what are often called "merit goods," things that the public thinks are desirable, but that would be provided insufficiently by private enterprise. Parks, libraries, and museums are examples.

A fourth kind of thing that is either government financed or controlled, or both, is the natural monopoly. Because the electric company, the gas company, and some others, operate systems where it is not feasible to have a number of competitors serving the same customers, the normal market mechanism cannot operate. In this situation the monopolist is free to charge what he wishes unless he is controlled by the government.

Aside from these four kinds of things, the free market economist usually does not favor government financing or operation. Specifi-

---

*The "invisible hand" metaphor characterizes the behavior of an unregulated economic system: the hand guides the system to produce only those items that people are willing to purchase at the price they are willing to pay.

cally, he does not favor government financing or operation merely on the basis of allegations that the government can provide the product or service more cheaply than private industry. In general, he believes that the sum of private decisions will be for the public good, and this is the point at which he disagrees with those who espouse a planned economy. If we are to adopt the viewpoint of the free market economists, we must ask ourselves whether higher education, and specifically community college education, falls in any of the four categories that qualify for government control or financing. If not, we must come to the conclusion that higher education should be private.

Certainly, higher education is not the same sort of thing as is national defense, where it is unfeasible to limit the benefits of it to those who choose to purchase it. It may be true that there are external benefits to higher education that benefit others than those who partake of the education. But so long as the returns to higher education for the individual are in excess of those one would be apt to get by other investments, there is no need to fear that no one would be willing to make a private investment in higher education.

Nor does higher education fall into the category of those things that require such a large investment that private industry would not make the necessary investment. The existence of many private institutions of higher education attests to this fact. While most private institutions receive some government subsidy, it amounts to only about 10 percent of revenue on the average for private two- and four-year colleges, and there are many proprietary (profit-making) institutions offering higher education curricula that receive no subsidy.

It can be argued that higher education is a merit good, one which would be insufficiently provided and consumed if it were not subsidized by the government, although many economists would dispute this allegation. Many educators point to the large postwar demand for college places, and the fact that the private institutions did not expand fast enough to provide for the demand. But this is something of a self-fulfilling hypothesis. So long as public institutions provided the places at less cost to the students than could private institutions, the demand for *private* college places was insufficient to stimulate the necessary investment. If, instead, there had been no public institutions, the production of college-trained personnel would have been insufficient at first to meet the demand. This would have increased the price employers were willing to pay for the services of college graduates, which would have increased the attractiveness of a college education, and therefore the willingness of private investors to provide the educational plant.

There are those who say instead that it is the duty of the colleges of our country, and particularly the public colleges, to assess the manpower needs of the country, and to provide college places and programs to train people to meet those manpower needs. Much of the rhetoric calling for increased money for higher education has been based on this premise. This manpower argument would be rejected by free-market economists. They would assert that the market system will automatically take care of the problem, and that such planning is an unwarranted interference in the market. It is the proponents of the planned economy who would favor this argument. Indeed, the provision of higher education in all of the communist countries and most of the underdeveloped world is planned on this basis. There is more discussion of the planned economy in the next chapter.

Even assuming that higher education is a merit good, and that the amount of external benefit is a measure of the amount of education that would not be undertaken by individuals interested only in their private benefit, we still do not have a guide to the amount of government support required. It is not correct to assume that, say, half of the benefits of higher education are external benefits, and to infer from that that half of the cost should be borne by government. Even assuming that we knew what proportion of the benefits accrue to society as a whole (which we don't), the correct remedy in a market model is to use only as much government subsidy as is necessary to stimulate the additional socially desired consumption of education above what would otherwise be consumed by individuals acting in their own self-interest. The additional government subsidization might turn out to be greater or less than would be implied by the ratio of external to private benefits, depending upon the elasticity of demand for education. It is interesting that this economic rule does not seem to be generally appreciated by those who would use the purported existence of substantial external benefits as a reason for substantial government subsidy.

Complicating this whole argument is the fact that there are some economists who believe that the external benefits of higher education are so little as to be unimportant in comparison to the private benefits, and thus believe that government subsidy should be limited to subsidization of poor students. For example, based on this premise, Lee Hansen and Burton Weisbrod of the University of Wisconsin have proposed that the state of Wisconsin limit its subsidization of higher education to vouchers that would be given to needy students, and that could be spent at any institution, public or private.[1] Direct payments to institutions by the state would cease.

This leads us to another sense in which education can be thought of as a merit good. That is the distribution argument. If education were completely private, and students paid in tuition all or most of the cost of being educated, there would be a class of students too poor to afford the education. If we agree that it is important for the great majority of our citizens to have some higher education (and as a society we long ago agreed to this at the elementary and secondary level), then monetary requirements that effectively prevent some parts of the population from obtaining one are not in the interest of the society. It is significant that the U. S. Supreme Court, in its decision in the *Rodriguez* case in Texas, noted that if tuition were charged in the elementary and secondary schools the case for upsetting the school finance laws of Texas would have been much stronger, because there would have been a clearly defined class of people who were *denied* an education (rather than simply provided one of lower quality). Free market economists will admit this is an argument, but insist that the problem should be taken care of by a system of grants to students who are needy, rather than by subsidizing institutions so they can provide low-cost education to needy and non-needy alike.

Finally, it is unlikely that education might be thought of as a natural monopoly. The presence of directly competing institutions in many cities shows clearly that it is not. Of course, it could be argued that the single institution of higher education that may exist in a smaller city is a natural monopoly in that city and its surrounding area, but that is the result of sparsity of population, and could apply equally to many other services in small cities, towns, and rural areas. Certainly, the local college does not occupy the same position as did the railroad before the advent of highways and trucking when trains were the only practical way in which goods could enter or leave small towns.

It appears then that, using the premises of the free market economists, public subsidization and control of education is not necessary, and is thereby undesirable. Distribution problems could be taken care of by government grants to students that could be spent at the college of their choice. This would eliminate both direct government subsidization and government control of institutions. Higher education would be completely private, and might be either non-profit or proprietary. Wherever entrepreneurs saw a sufficient demand, they would establish colleges or programs within colleges. Those who were offering programs for which there was insufficient demand, or which operated inefficiently, would languish and ultimately fail.

Perhaps the best argument against the market-economy model of higher education (without using the arguments of those who favor the planned economy) is the existence of market imperfections, which are the differences between the real world and the theoretical models of the economists. The free market idea presumes the existence of informed buyers, who will compare quality and price of goods and services offered, and choose those that offer the combination of quality and price that best suits them. To the extent that buyers are not properly informed, they operate in the dark and the market does not work properly. This has been one of the problems of our modern economy, where each manufacturer does his best to differentiate his product from other similar products, through extensive advertising of differences that are often minor and cosmetic. Each manufacturer thus hopes to create a limited monopoly for himself, so that he can better control the price at which he sells.

Market imperfections hamper the distribution of the products and services of higher education as well as those of the rest of the economy: it is difficult to get adequate information about institutions or the programs they offer and there is reason to believe that the advertising that would exist under a completely private system would do more to obfuscate things than to illuminate them. A partial solution to this (and something that might be very desirable regardless of the type of financing plan adopted) might be to have a central source of uniform information for potential students about all of higher education—public and private, two- and four-year. This information depository might be operated by the government, or by a respected nonprofit agency similar to the present accrediting agencies. Each institution that wished to be eligible for government aid (including the enrollment of students receiving education grants or loans) would be required to submit standardized information about a variety of things that would be helpful to the prospective student in choosing his college.

Such an information depository would include information on the faculty's qualifications and achievements, the courses and programs offered, tuition and fees, requirements for degrees and credentials, description of the physical plant, percentage of students who complete programs, and a record of the success those who completed programs had in finding jobs in the field for which they trained. In addition to this, the college could have some latitude in making a statement about what it believes its strengths or unique characteristics to be. The statements of the college would be subject to audit and verification by the agency that is custodian of the information. This information bank would be computerized. A prospective student would be able, for a small fee, to specify characteristics of the type of educational institution or program in which he was interested. Computer analysis would allow him to receive promptly information on the five or 10 institutions that most closely fitted his specifications.

Of course, this would not prevent institutions from advertising in whatever ways they saw fit (subject to the truth-in-advertising laws), but the existence of the standardized data source would make it possible for students to get material that would allow them to make a valid comparison among possible colleges.

Another kind of market imperfection arises from the long lead time necessary to prepare people for careers. In the late 1950s the nation decided that it was necessary to prepare many physicists to enable us to overtake Russia in the space race. We poured many millions of dollars into this, and by the late 1960s many physicists were pouring out of the end of the pipeline, only to find that the nation was no longer very interested in space. This lead-time problem has been pointed to by the manpower planners as a reason for adopting their ideas. It is assumed by them that individuals will react, in deciding on college programs, to the immediate prospect for jobs in their chosen field, rather than the prospect when they complete college. The argument is attractive, but the facts do not bear it out. The experience of the nation with the production of physicists shows that government may do no better than individuals in predicting the future. And the rapidity with which students have transferred out of programs in education as the market became saturated brings renewed faith in the validity of individual decisions.

Market Economy Models

There are three main variations of the market-economy model of higher education: the completely private system with no government aid, a private system in which government grants are given to individual students, and a private system in which grants from government bodies are available to individual colleges. All three models and how well each meets the nine criteria established in the preceding chapter, will be discussed in the following sections.

The Completely Private System

A completely private system would represent the market economy in its purest sense. All institutions would be private, and would neither be controlled nor subsidized in any way by any government body. There would be no indirect subsidies through grants to students and no such thing as a source of standardized information. There are at present a few private, nonprofit institutions operating in the United States that would fit this model and perhaps most of the proprietary (profit-making) institutions would also fit it. However, the model does not work as it would in its pure form because private institutions are in competition with other institutions that receive substantial government subsidization, and this distorts the operation of the market system.

If we can imagine such a system operating throughout higher education, we could ask ourselves how, with respect to community colleges, the system would meet the criteria for judging finance plans.

1. *Serve those otherwise not well served.* In some ways it would clearly impede the ability of the community college (or whatever its concomitant might be under such a completely private system) to serve those who find access to traditional institutions difficult. With all colleges charging sufficient tuition to cover the cost of instruction, and no grants to needy students, the poor and even many of those of the lower middle-income group would find it impossible to afford college. While institutions and philanthropies might provide some money for student aid, it is doubtful that the amount provided would meet more than a fraction of the need.

On the other hand, it is possible that a completely private system might enhance the ability to provide for some of the other groups that find access to traditional institutions difficult. Without low-tuition competition from public community colleges, private entrepreneurs might find it worthwhile to provide programs that would meet the needs of those of lower ability, those who live some distance from traditional institutions, and those who are beyond the traditional college age. But they would do this only if they found students who were able to pay for their own education.

2. *Provide programs otherwise not provided.* A completely private system, other things being equal, should enhance the provision of courses and programs not provided, or insufficiently provided, by traditional institutions for under such a system, if there is sufficient demand for a program (regardless of whether it is "traditional"), there would be an incentive for entrepreneurs to provide it, again presuming the ability of the students to pay for it.

3. *Respond to community needs.* For the same reason, a completely private system would presumably enhance the provision of courses and programs that meet the needs of the local community, for it is the business of the private entrepreneur to figure out what the market wants and provide it. However, we must insert here a major caveat with regard to both criteria 2 and 3: private enterprise will provide what the public wants only if the public is able adequately to evaluate what it is going to get when it buys. Otherwise, there would be a tendency for the entrepreneur to provide a less expensive substitute for what the public thinks it is getting. And the difficulties to the potential buyer of evaluating educational institutions and programs are much greater than those of evaluating various models

of automobiles. Provision of an information bank such as has been suggested above might help alleviate the problem, but under this pure model such provision would be unwarranted interference by government.

There is another problem regarding the way this model meets this criterion. It is that there is no way to express *community* preferences. Only private preferences are reflected in the marketplace. If there are external benefits in a community college education, it is desirable that there be a mechanism for the public to express its preferences.

4. *Help preserve the private sector.* A completely private system would completely satisfy the criterion of keeping the private sector of higher education healthy. Of course, some particular private institutions might not survive, but this would be because they were not meeting the needs of the public or were operated inefficiently.

5. *Keep expansion within bounds.* A completely private system would certainly keep expansion of the community colleges within the bounds of public willingness to support them, for this is one of the major virtues of the market system. And it would not be necessary to take into account the financial health of state and local governments because the institutions would make no demands upon them.

6. *Inter-institutional efficiency.* A completely private system would not prevent duplication among the levels of education. Since there would be no control of programs, any institution could offer any program if it desired to do so. However, a private system might do a rather good job of preventing wasteful duplication, for duplication that was not economically demanded would soon cease for lack of support. This also is a major virtue of the market system. In essence, those who believe in the market system would dismiss this criterion as unnecessary.

7. *Intra-institutional efficiency.* A completely private system would clearly encourage the various institutions to operate their own programs efficiently. Because they must compete on the open market with other institutions, the one that operates most efficiently will be the most vigorous. The incentives in private industry are toward efficient operation except where a natural monopoly exists, and it was argued earlier that education does not constitute a natural monopoly.

8. *Equity to students.* A completely private system would not provide equity to students, in the sense of the *Serrano* criterion. The private community college in a free market economy would be almost entirely supported by tuition and would have to gear its program to the ability to pay of those it served. This would result in low cost and low quality colleges in poor areas, and high cost, high quality colleges in richer areas; a pattern that now exists, both among

private and public institutions. Under a completely private system there would be no way to correct this inequity, and the supporters of such a system would think it undesirable to do so.

9. *Equity to taxpayers.* A completely private system would provide equity to the taxpayers, because they would not be paying taxes to support it.

The major positive features of a completely private system are the promotion of greater variety in institutions and programs, automatic regulation of the amount of education provided, encouragement of efficient operation, and a lessened burden to the taxpayers. The major drawbacks are the lack of equity for students, both in a geographic and economic sense, and the danger that the profit motive would encourage the provision of educational programs that gave the appearance, rather than the reality, of quality and of meeting the needs of the students. In spite of the positive features, these drawbacks are probably so great that few would recommend this purest form of the market-economy model for all of higher education or for all of community college education. But examples of this model do exist in the United States at the present time, perhaps more in the proprietary sector than in the private, nonprofit sector. There are private institutions that receive all, or almost all, of their support from private sources, both tuition and philanthropic. These institutions cannot, in general, compete directly with the low-tuition public community colleges. They have survived by offering environments, programs, or courses that are not offered by the community colleges. In other words, in those limited areas in which they have specialized, they have outdone the community colleges at their own game. They have provided educational offerings that are not provided, or are not provided in the form the public wants, by the community colleges.

Private System With Government Grants to Students

A less pure form of the market economy model would be one in which institutions would receive no government money directly, but in which there would be government subsidization of students, on a selective or nonselective basis. If done on a selective basis, the subsidy would be used to promote certain social goals, such as providing access to higher education for needy students. If done on a nonselective basis, the system would approximate what has been called a "social security" type plan: a payroll tax used to entitle each person to the equivalent of two (or four) years of post-secondary education, with the education to be acquired all at one time, or in bits and pieces throughout an individual's life as one felt the need for it. In either case, one would be free to use one's grant at any educational institution desired (including proprietary ones), as was done with the G. I. Bill. Of course, it would be necessary to provide some form of investigation to be sure that "institutions" were not being set up for the purpose of defrauding the government. This necessary government intervention might well be combined with the information bank described earlier. But control of institutions would still be completely private, and they would be free to offer any sort of educational experience that was desired by students.

Examples of private institutions that fit this model exist in almost all states, for the federal government provides student aid that may be used by students attending private institutions, and many states have similar aid plans. As with the completely private plan, the existence of institutions that fit this model does not mean that it works as intended because it now must compete with government-subsidized institutions.

This plan retains many of the desirable features of the first model while it eliminates or alleviates some of the latter's undesirable features. As compared with the private plan, this second model could better serve those otherwise not well served through the use of selective grants based on financial need. And it might reduce the lack of adequate information for the student as consumer, which constitutes a significant market imperfection through use of the computerized evaluation system.

A model of this type has been proposed by some economists and it is attractive. However, it has yet to be demonstrated that the guiding hand of the market as expressed in the sum of private decisions will provide us with all that we, as a nation, feel we need in the way of higher education. The market works very well where it is easy to evaluate the worth of a product or service. But the outputs of education are diverse and often difficult to evaluate. In this situation, the profit motive does not coincide well with the needs in all cases. This particularly tends to be so with things we might classify as "cultural," as a look at the offerings of television will corroborate. On the other hand, it is possible that the private sector would do a very good job of offering the sort of vocational training that prepares people for specific jobs. In many cases the proprietary sector is doing that now and surviving in spite of competiton from the community colleges.

Although this private system with government grants to students has many attractive features, it probably cannot serve as the only model for American higher education. But it is worth trying to incorporate its best features into an overall plan. These are the possibility of government subsidization of students on the basis of selective grants or else the "social security" approach, which would guarantee all Americans the right to, say, the equivalent of two years of post-secondary education. The social security approach could satisfy the criterion of equity to the student if it indeed guarantees to each person some free education at the college of his choice. But the cost of such a program would be exceedingly high. This would make it politically necessary to restrict the amount guaranteed to each student to less than the cost of the education. Poor students would be restricted in their rights to an education in order to guarantee some money to richer students who could have afforded it anyway. This is an inefficient but politically attractive way to do things.

Private System with Government Grants to Institutions

This model would have all of the institutions private, but would have some direct government subsidization of institutions. The subsidization would be on a formula basis that would (supposedly) not interfere with the institution's right to spend it as it wished. One such system is that currently in effect in New York, where private institutions are paid by the state: $800 for each bachelor's degree awarded, $600 for each master's, and $3,000 for each doctoral degree. In a sense, this is a system of revenue sharing, in which government gives unrestricted money to the private institutions. There are two serious drawbacks to the idea. One has to do with the distribution criteria, the other with government control.

In order to have a revenue sharing system, it is necessary to establish criteria for deciding which institutions receive money, and how much each shall get. It is almost inevitable that distribution would be limited to institutions already established. It is usually difficult for institutions to qualify for government grants when they are so innovative that their structure is significantly different from those that already exist. (These same things also make it difficult for such an institution to be approved by one of the accrediting agencies, and it is likely that accreditation would be used as one requirement for receiving grants. In addition, if accreditation were used as a criterion, proprietary institutions would, at present, be completely excluded, for the accrediting agencies refuse to accredit them.) On the other hand, it would appear that, under the proposed plan, an accredited institution could receive the government money regardless of its quality or efficiency.

As a basis for determining how much each college would receive, it is clear that the New York formula would not benefit community colleges, for it pays for nothing below the bachelor's degree. Payment might, instead, have to be based on number of credit-hours of courses offered, which would be likely to discourage innovation. Another need not met by the New York plan is how to give financial aid to reward the important community service functions of the community colleges.

The other principal problem with this model has to do with government control. The idea behind grants to institutions under this plan is that they should be made on the basis of an objective formula and have no strings attached, an idea that is probably unrealistic. It is just not reasonable to expect politicians, responsible as they are to the electorate, to continue for very long to give money to private institutions to spend as they wish with no control. All that would be necessary would be for a few examples of unwise expenditure of the governmental allocations to come to light, and the government would insist on some controls. Over time, these controls would become more and more stringent, and ultimately the whole idea of unrestricted funds and a hands-off attitude by the government would be lost.

This model would be similar to the completely private system in the way it meets the first three criteria: serving those otherwise not well served, providing programs not otherwise provided, and responding to community needs. Grants to institutions would not necessarily guarantee access to poor students, so the market models continue to meet the first criterion somewhat poorly. This model is better able than the completely private model to respond to community needs because the institutional grants would give schools some money to meet these needs that would not have to come from tuition. But there is no assurance that it will use this money for community needs.

The model would meet the fourth criterion, of preserving the health of the private sector, for this is what it is quite clearly designed to do. It does not meet the fifth criterion, keeping expansion within bounds, for it is an open-ended claim on the state treasury. There is no mechanism, under this model, for limiting the number of degrees or credit-hours, or whatever, on which claims could be submitted. The only way the state could control this drain, then, would be to decrease the allowance per unit claimed, which would upset the budgets of the institutions that had planned on the funds being taken away from them.

This model does nothing about the sixth criterion, prevention of wasteful duplication among levels and institutions of education. But, as was noted earlier, this is presumed to be unnecessary in the market-economy model, where the forces of the marketplace will take care of the problem. However, to the extent that governmental subsidy makes it possible for institutions to survive that otherwise would not, the forces of the marketplace are muted. Therefore, this model would not meet this criterion as well as would the other two market-economy models. The same can be said of the way it meets the seventh criterion, that of intra-institutional efficiency, and for the same reason. The model does a somewhat better job of meeting the eighth criterion, of equity (in the *Serrano* sense) to the student, for the institutional subsidies would tend to reduce the differences in income between colleges in poor communities and those in rich communities, and thus reduce the differences in the quality of education provided. But the improvement would probably be rather small unless the institutional subsidies were so large as to make the colleges quasi-public. Finally, since the model assumes that all subsidies would come from state or federal governments, it meets the ninth criterion of equity to the taxpayers, for these subsidies come from general tax revenue; they would be raised at a uniform rate from all taxpayers of the state, and thus would not discriminate geographically like local property taxes.

In summary, this model seems to have several drawbacks that would not exist for a private system with grants to students, and no compensating positive features. About all that can be said for it is that it is attractive to private institutions currently facing financial problems, and to those in states where they have the political power to convince the legislature that it would cost less to subsidize existing private institutions than to have them fail and then have to provide public institutions to take their place.

CHAPTER IV

Financing Community Colleges: Planned Economy and Mixed Models

BECAUSE the United States has primarily a market economy in the private sector, we sometimes fail to realize the extent to which elements of our public sector resemble the planned economies of the communist countries. This resemblance is particularly striking in activities such as education, where public sector and private sector activity exist side by side. A comparison of the differing goals and methods of operation of the two systems will highlight this dichotomy.

The market economy uses the market as the great regulator of economic activity; the planned economy denies the market this function. Instead, the planned economy is planned centrally, with government dictating what shall be produced, the quantity and quality to be produced, where it is to be distributed, and the price at which it is to be sold. There are virtues and faults to each system; naturally the proponents of each magnify its virtues and minimize its faults.

The principal virtues of the planned economy are alleged to be the elimination of wasteful duplication of effort, and of frivolous or harmful production. Production is designed to satisfy the goals of the state instead of assuming, as in the market economy, that the sum of individual decisions will automatically confer the greatest good on society as a whole. The faults of the planned economy are purported to lie in two areas: lack of individual choice, and lack of efficiency. In the planned economy, the existence of a consumer demand for products does not mean that these products will be produced, unless their production agrees with the state plan. It is contended that there is a drab sameness about the products that one may purchase, and that many amenities are unavailable. Efficiency is lacking, it is contended, because planners are unable to plan adequately in the detail that is necessary, and the result is shortages of some things and gluts of others.

Planned Economy Models

Some current community college systems strongly resemble the planned economies, with both their achievements and their problems—the prototype being the community college system completely controlled by the state. In such a system, there is no local financial contribution and the administration of each college is responsible to a central state board. Educational goals for the system are centrally decided, with each campus told how many students it shall have, and what courses and programs it shall offer. A detailed budget for each college is approved centrally by the board or by the legislature, line item by line item, with movement of funds between line items difficult or impossible. Complex methods of budgeting and control are emphasized. There is little opportunity for those involved locally to shape the institution to meet local needs, and the red tape required by central authority seems endless. The goals of serving the needs of the state and of elimination of wasteful duplication and frivolous courses have been served, but at the expense of a diminution of consumer choice and possible inefficiency.

Two finance models based on the idea of the planned economy are discussed below.

State Financing with Centralized Control

A completely centralized system would, of course, be the purest form of the planned economy model. Individual colleges would be, in effect, branch campuses of a centrally controlled, statewide, community college system. The budget would be established by a state board on a line-item basis. There would be no local financial contribution and no mechanism for local decision-making on programs. Some colleges might specialize in some programs and other colleges in different programs, but the decisions as to which programs would be emphasized would be made by the central board. Students would apply for entry to the community college system, and while most would attend the college in their local community, they could instead be assigned by the state board to a different campus in order to achieve efficient utilization of facilities. Tuition would be neither necessary nor proscribed. If charged, the amounts would be based on rules that were uniform throughout the system, although it would be possible to charge amounts that differed according to ability to pay or cost of program.

It is probably an oversimplification to attempt to categorize the public community college system of any state into any one of the models discussed in this book, for no system exists in the pure form conceived of in these models. Nevertheless, in order to get some idea of the variety of financing systems for community colleges that exist in the United States, a survey was taken in 1973 of those responsible for community college systems in the states. The survey, made with the cooperation of the American Association of Community and Junior Colleges, requested information on the form of financing public community colleges in the state as of that date and on financial data for the year 1971-72. Replies were received from 36 states and Puerto Rico, which represents 96 percent of the public community college enrollment of the United States. In this survey, each state was asked to provide printed material or explain in general the system of financing the public community colleges of the state, particularly regarding the determination of state and local fiscal contributions. On the basis of the replies (some in great detail, some unfortunately too brief) an attempt has been made to place the state systems into the categories or models. Recognizing that this does represent an oversimplification, and that the classification has at times been made with insufficient knowledge, the insights gained are still useful.

None of the state systems of public community colleges would be classified into one of the three market-economy models, for these models all envision private institutions. The classification of some state systems into the centralized state-controlled model has been done on the basis of inferences about the system from questionnaire replies about its financing. Essentially, if the finance involves little or no local contribution, and if the state amount to each college is determined on the basis of direct appropriation or allocation based on an approved budget, it was assumed that the state's system falls into this category. On this basis, Alaska, Colorado (the six state-operated colleges), Georgia, Iowa, Kentucky, Massachusetts, Montana, Oklahoma, Utah, Virginia, Rhode Island, and Puerto Rico have centralized, state-controlled systems. Massachusetts perhaps represents the clearest example of the model. (See Appendix Three for a description of each of these state's financing systems.)

This model meets the criteria for finance systems in a variety of ways. It is probably positive with regard to the first criterion, that of offering access to those finding access to the traditional institutions difficult. In fact, to the extent that central control could result in more efficient allocation of funds, it is possible that the criterion could be better met under a centralized system.

This model does not meet the second criterion, of providing programs otherwise not provided, for the lack of incentive for innovation and the tendency toward uniformity discourage a school from offering any programs that differ from the norm. This model does not meet the third criterion well either. Centralized state control, and the lack of a local financial contribution, both act to restrict a community's ability to see to it that its college offers programs the community feels it needs. Although there can be community advisory councils or similar organizations, the effect is not the same as when the representatives of the local community have real power. A tendency toward uniformity and a lack of innovation are the main drawbacks of this model.

Nor does this model help preserve the health of the private sector of post-secondary education, the fourth criterion. On the other hand, it meets the fifth criterion well, that of keeping expansion within bounds. With a centralized system, the budget of the community college system becomes, in effect, part of the overall state budget. The amounts to be expended are thrashed out politically in the governor's office and the legislature, and the appropriations constitute the total of the system's claims on the state treasury. The state faces no unpleasant surprises resulting from unanticipated claims by the system.

The centralized system does meet criterion six well: it prevents wasteful duplication among the institutions and levels of education in the state because the amount of duplication or overlap can be easily regulated by the state. On the other hand, the model meets the seventh criterion poorly: it discourages efficient operation of each individual college. The system of line-item budgeting and appropriations based on approved budgets insures the existence of a phenomenon common to all state agencies. Each college overstates its budget needs, assuming they will be cut at the state level. And a budget is never underspent on the assumption that if a school spends less than was appropriated, its appropriation will be cut the next year. In addition, it is usually impossible to carry over a saving to the next year, for unexpended funds usually revert to the state treasury. As a result, there is a frantic effort made at the end of the fiscal year to be sure that all unexpended amounts are encumbered. The system suffers, as do the planned economies of eastern Europe, from the fact that the market mechanism is not operating, and the controls that are used as a substitute are often not effective.

This model should well serve the eighth criterion, that of equity to the student. With a centrally controlled and financed system, there should not be the differences in quality among colleges that there are in some other systems; it would therefore meet the *Serrano* criterion. Finally, this model provides equity to the taxpayers, since it is financed out of the general fund of the state, and thus does not constitute a heavier burden on the residents of one community than on those of another. However, this equity only exists if the community colleges are appropriately sited so that most residents of the state who pay taxes for their support have access to their services.

In summary, the centralized system tends, more than do most models, to provide equity to students and taxpayers, to keep the monetary demands of the community colleges on the state treasury within bounds, and to prevent wasteful duplication. But it does this at the expense of being less responsive to local needs, of ignoring the private sector, and of having inadequate mechanisms for promoting efficient operation.

State Financing with Some Decentralization of Control

This model assumes, as does the previous one, that there will be little or no local financial contribution to community colleges, but it attempts to ameliorate some of the problems of the previous model by allowing individual colleges to have some say in how they spend their money. This obviously implies a substantial reduction in the central government's role of budgetary approval, which means that another mechanism must be found for distributing the state money. The answer lies in some form of formula budgeting, where state money is allocated on the basis of more or less complicated formulas that relate to the needs of the college. These formulas may allocate instructional personnel, for example, on the basis of one for every 20 full-time equivalent or FTE* students. The local college hires the personnel, and the money allocated for their salaries is based on the placement of these personnel on a state salary schedule. Allocations for janitorial service may be based on the number of square feet of building space, and allowances for instructional materials on the basis of a certain number of dollars per FTE. The system may become very complicated (that of North Carolina is an example, see Appendix Three).

A different approach is that used in Florida, where all programs are placed into one of four expense categories, ranging from business and liberal arts courses (least expensive) to certain vocational courses that are most expensive. An allowance per FTE is established for each of the four categories, based on cost studies, and the community colleges are entitled to state money calculated by multi-

---

*FTE stands for "full-time equivalent." Because many of the students in community colleges attend on a part-time basis, counting the number of students enrolled is an unsatisfactory way to estimate the instructional load. Most institutions use the concept of full-time equivalent students as a measure of instructional load, although the method of calculating it varies from state to state. A typical method is to assume that a full-time course load is 15 units, then the total number of units (or "student hours") of enrollment is divided by 15 to give the number of FTE students.

plying the number of FTE enrolled in each category by the allowance for the category. In the case of either type of formula, the emphasis in this model is on state allocations based on a formula, thus lessening the need for centralized state control of budgeting and program. As in the centralized model, there would be little or no local contribution. The states that appear to have systems that fit into this model are Connecticut, Florida, North Carolina, South Carolina, Tennessee, and Washington, with those of Florida and Tennessee fitting most closely.

The main differences between this model and the completely centralized model are that this one fosters some innovation (criterion two), and increases the ability of the college to respond to the needs of the community in which it is located (criterion three), at the expense of making the demands of the system upon the state treasury less definite (criterion five) and increasing the possibility of wasteful duplication (criterion six). Aside from these, both models have similar strengths and weaknesses.

A word is in order regarding the two types of formula approaches typified by those of North Carolina and Florida. The detailed system used in North Carolina provides a formula for practically every line item in the budget in an attempt to provide an objective formula that meets the needs of the individual colleges. The concept is good, but it is based on the assumption that each of the formulas is accurately related to the cost of the service to which it relates. The more formulas there are, though, the less likely it is that they will be closely scrutinized at frequent intervals to see that this is so: colleges would soon find out which formulas were overgenerous and would find ways to qualify for these allowances. In addition, the detailed formulas imply equalities in costs among colleges where such equalities do not exist. For example, the North Carolina system goes to the detail of allowing $400 for travel for the business manager of the college. The business manager of the college located in the capital may have little need for a travel allowance; one located across the state from the capital may need a good deal more than $400. In other words, the method of formula budgeting that develops the formulas on a line-item basis implies a spurious accuracy that often results in inequitable allocations and in manipulation of accounts by the college.

The type of formula budgeting typified by Florida's method represents a distinct improvement on the line-item formulas, although it too has some drawbacks. The idea is to classify programs into a limited number of cost categories, and base allocation formulas on average statewide costs for the categories determined from accurate cost studies. This approach avoids the rigidities and spurious accuracy of the line-item approach, and also makes it much easier for both the state and each college to estimate in advance the amount of the allocations. In addition, the money in the allocations may be used for any college purpose, so that restrictions on transfers among line items are not the problem they often are with the other system. Thus, this method gives the local college a good deal more budgeting freedom than does the other.

One problem with this approach has to do with the difficulties of classifying FTE by program. In most cases, this would be done by classifying courses by program and then counting credit-hours registered in each course. There will be a tendency to design low-cost courses that can be classified into high-cost categories, and then require these courses of all students in certain programs. Another problem is that the fewer the number of cost categories, the more likely it is that certain courses or programs will be badly overfunded or underfunded. On the other hand, if the number of cost classifications is expanded greatly, the problem of correct classification of courses is multiplied, and the difficulty and cost of regular cost studies increases. The number of program cost categories should probably range from five to 10 to provide a reasonable number of categories without making the system unwieldy. All in all, however, it appears that the formula budgeting approach using program cost classifications is a better approach than the line-item formula budgeting approach.

The Mixed Models

The market-economy model and the planned-economy model represent opposite extremes. While examples of both exist in the United States (one in the private sector and one in the public), it is evident that in most of the states the public has been unwilling to go for either of these extremes. The market-economy model represents complete freedom to determine locally what to offer (that is, the colleges offer what the consumers will buy) at the expense of any statewide coordination or control. The planned-economy model offers coordinated statewide effort toward state-determined goals at the expense of a loss of local control and of efficiency.

The models to be discussed in this section represent a kind of middle ground between the extremes. The thing that characterizes them all is the existence of a financial (and control) partnership between the state government and a local government. Systems fitting these models, then, would be public institutions. The idea of the state-local partnership is to enhance the influence of the local community in the determination of program, so the program can meet the needs of the local community as decided by that community. This is criterion three, and the name "community college" implies that this criterion is very important. The four models discussed below are distinguished from one another by the manner in which the amounts of the state and local shares are determined.

Percentage Matching

States using this method usually allow the local community college to set its own budget as desired. The state then agrees to provide a percentage of this budget (e.g., one-third, as in Pennsylvania). The remainder is to be made up from other sources, mostly tuition and local taxation or appropriation. The state may specify the percentage that is to come from each of the other sources (in Pennsylvania, one-third from local sources).

There are five states (of the 36 plus Puerto Rico in the sample) whose system is percentage-matching in form: Maryland, Missouri, New Jersey, New York, and Pennsylvania. However, because the form of this model implies a blank check on the state treasury, most states have been forced to set a maximum on the state's participation. Where this maximum is set too low, most colleges will receive the maximum, and the effect is that of a flat grant; at least this appears to be the case in four of the five states with percentage matching. Only in Pennsylvania does the system appear to operate in a pure fashion.

The intent of the percentage-matching method is to encourage community colleges to provide what is needed in their localities without interference from the state. The state merely agrees to shoulder part of the cost. Let us examine the model in the light of the criteria.

Provision of access to those who find access to traditional institutions difficult (criterion one) is affected negatively by percentage matching because those areas containing the largest proportion of such students tend to be poor areas. They can raise less money locally, and thus get less from the state, and so are unable to offer the variety or quality of programs offered by colleges in the wealthy areas.

The model meets well the second and third criteria, of providing programs otherwise not provided and responding to community needs. Because the state contribution is not tied to FTE or credit-hours, there is no artificial restriction on courses or programs that do not fit easily into the traditional mold. And local determination of the budget (with a percentage of that budget raised locally) insures that the program will be designed to meet needs as locally defined.

This model (in common with all of the models in this group, and the two planned-economy models) does not meet criterion four, preserving the health and independence of the private sector. The market-economy models, on the other hand, meet the criterion with a completely private system. Since it is unlikely that any state would go to a completely market model, it will be necessary to discuss later ways in which adjustments can be made in the other models to help meet this criterion.

A serious failing of this model is its inability to meet the fifth criterion, that of keeping the state's expenditures for its community colleges within the bounds of its ability and willingness to support them. In its pure form, the model implies a completely open-ended commitment by the state. All that is necessary for the local college is to decide on the size of its budget, and the state will pick up a percentage of it. This is the kind of commitment that gives state treasurers and politicians nightmares, and most states have found it necessary to set limits on this state matching. The limit usually takes the form of a maximum number of dollars per FTE that will be provided by the state. If this limit were sufficiently high, the principle of percentage matching would not be seriously compromised. But in four of the five states where the system is percentage matching in principle, it is not so to any great extent in fact. As the budgets of the colleges have expanded rapidly, the limit has increased more slowly. The result is that the majority of the colleges are receiving, not a percentage of their budgets, but a fixed number of dollars per FTE from the state. Their system is, in effect, a flat-grant method (discussed below). Only in Pennsylvania is the principle that one-third of the budget shall come from the state adhered to closely.

The percentage-matching system does nothing to satisfy criterion six, that of inter-institutional efficiency. The reasoning that works in favor of local determination of program works against prevention of duplication. But it does provide an incentive for the colleges to operate their programs efficiently, (which is criterion seven), at least more than there is in the planned-economy models (and probably less than there is in the market-economy models). The incentive comes from the fact that the budget is locally determined and a portion of it locally raised. The college is free to spend this money as it sees fit, and the more efficiently it does this, the more it will be able to satisfy its local constituency while keeping taxes down. But this kind of incentive is clearly not as strong an incentive as that of the private system, where one competes or fails.

The percentage-matching system fails to meet the eighth and ninth criteria, those of equity to the student and to the taxpayer. These imply that the amount of money available per student at a college should not be a function of the wealth of the local community, and that taxpayers in one community should not have to make a greater tax effort than taxpayers in another community in order to support similar programs. The percentage-matching system works directly against these. In the wealthy community a relatively low tax rate raises a large amount of money per student at the college. Because it has raised a large amount, the college will be entitled to a large amount from the state. In the poor community, a much higher tax rate may raise fewer dollars per student, thus entitling the college to fewer dollars from the state. Though the poorer community makes a greater tax effort, it must offer a lower quality program, and the state does nothing to remedy this, but instead reinforces it. The *Rodriguez* suit might have impressed the Supreme Court if such a system had been in effect in Texas. But in no state is the percentage-sharing system used for financing elementary and secondary schools. Only in the community colleges can a system with this perverse effect be found.

In summary, the percentage sharing model caters strongly to the right of the local community college to serve its community in the way it and its community see fit. It does this at the expense of issuing a blank check on the state treasury and of violating the criteria of equity to students and to taxpayers.

Flat Grant

This model has the state giving each college a grant based on a set number of dollars per FTE student. The college then raises the rest of its budget as it can, through local taxation, tuition, or otherwise. In the purest form of this model, the state would set no limitations on expansion of FTE in the colleges, or on either the tuition rate or the maximum local tax rate. The primary control would rest with the local college and its locally elected or appointed board. The money received through this flat grant could be used for any legitimate purpose by the college. Rather than a single set figure per FTE, the state could grant a certain number of dollars per academic FTE and a different, higher number of dollars per vocational FTE. The FTE could even be grouped by course into cost categories, with the grant per FTE in each category being related to (i.e., a percent of) the average statewide cost of courses in that category. This model would then resemble the system used in Florida (a decentralized, state-financed system), except in that state there is no financial partnership between the state and the locality—all of the money is furnished by the state (exclusive of tuition) under the formula. Under a flat-grant system, the locality furnishes a substantial portion of the operating money.

Nine states in the sample of 36 plus Puerto Rico have a formula that is flat grant in form: Colorado (the six locally operated colleges), Kansas, Mississippi, New Mexico, North Dakota, Oregon, Texas, and Wisconsin. Another six states have a formula that in form is like another model, but because the limitations imposed by the state are artificially low, the theoretical model operates so that most colleges get a maximum or minimum grant expressed in terms of a set number of dollars per FTE (or similar unit), and thus have, in effect, a flat-grant system. These states include Illinois, Maryland, Michigan, Missouri, New Jersey, and New York. (See Appendix Three for description of these plans.)

The flat-grant model is another way in which states have attempted to give community colleges money without dictating the content of their programs. It would do better than the percentage-matching plan on the first criterion, serving those to whom access is difficult, for it would allow at least a minimum program to all on an equal basis, but it would not do as well as the foundation or power-equalizing models in this respect. It does not do as well as the percentage-matching model meeting criteria two and three, those of providing programs otherwise not provided and responding to community needs. Although it avoids direct state control of the curriculum (as does percentage-matching), this model allows the state to exert an indirect influence on programs. If the distribution method involves only a single flat-grant amount per FTE, the college tends to offer the less expensive academic and business education courses, and to shun the more expensive vocational and technical courses. The best way to make the state neutral in this respect is to provide a different flat-grant amount for each program, with the amount paid per FTE for the program proportional to the actual cost of operating such a program. Of course, if the cost factors used are not updated periodically colleges will tend to find those that happen to be too high, for they will find it to their advantage to offer such courses and siphon off the money not needed in the program to underfunded programs they feel are locally desirable. Having a multiplicity of cost factors lessens one of the other desirable features of the flat-grant method: being able to predict fairly accurately how much the program will cost the state in the next fiscal year. Now, instead of having merely to predict overall state FTE (which can usually be predicted quite accurately), it is necessary to predict the number of FTE in each of a number of programs.

Another problem is that basing the flat grant on FTE may inhibit the offering of nontraditional educational experiences, for fear that these will not qualify to be counted in FTE, or will be inadequately counted.

As with all of the mixed models, this model does nothing to help keep private colleges financially healthy, which is the fourth criterion. It poses less of a danger to the state treasury, criterion five, than does the percentage-matching model, but still leaves open the problem that colleges are free to expand their enrollment without state permission, and thus qualify for more state aid. In common with the other mixed models, there is no mechanism in this model to prevent wasteful duplication of offerings, as called for by criterion six. This model, with its local control and opportunity to vary the local tax rate, has some incentives toward intra-institutional efficiency, the seventh criterion. In this respect, it does less well than the market-economy models and better than the planned-economy models.

The flat-grant method of distribution of state money tends in some measure to equalize educational opportunity and to provide equity to the taxpayer; the last two criteria, and in this respect it is theoretically better than the percentage-matching method. On the other hand, the flat-grant system implies more state influence (if not control) over the colleges than does the percentage-matching system. Percentage matching, aside from setting a maximum participation rate and perhaps defining some courses or programs that do not qualify for matching grants from the state, does not imply state interference in local program decisions. The setting of a maximum rate of state participation does imply a state-mandated method of counting and reporting FTE.

The flat-grant system does not *require* more in the way of state regulation than mandating the method of counting and reporting FTE. But as explained earlier, the flat grant exercises its influence. If there is only one flat-grant rate, colleges will tend to offer lower cost courses. If there are a number of rates, they will tend to concentrate on those programs whose rates are higher than costs warrant. And if the state attempts to circumvent these tendencies by frequently updating the cost factors, a state-mandated cost-accounting system must be instituted to accumulate the necessary cost information.

Foundation Program

The foundation program is a method of state and local sharing of current educational costs that emphasizes evening out the differences in a community's fiscal ability to support a community college. The method is in extensive use in elementary-secondary education, with more than half of the states using this method at that level. In essence, the state sets a certain number of dollars per FTE as representing the amount or *foundation* necessary for an adequate community college program (different numbers of dollars may be set for different programs). The state also specifies a local tax effort that must be made (usually in terms of a required tax rate), and may specify a tuition rate. The amount of the budget guaranteed by the state is equal to the foundation amount per FTE times the FTE of the college. From this is deducted the amount raised by the required local tax rate and the income from tuition, if any. The remainder is supplied by the state. There are four states whose state aid program is foundation in form: California, Illinois, Michigan and Wyoming. In addition, Montana's program *may* be this type. (See Appendix Three.)

The foundation model is probably better than the flat grant with regard to the first criterion, that of making access easy, because the amount uniformly provided tends to be higher. In meeting the second criterion (providing programs otherwise not provided) it suffers from the use of FTE students as a measure of need, and this may inhibit the offering of innovative programs whose costs are not reflected in the FTEs they generate.

The third criterion, of responding to community needs, is met well, because the foundation program implies the opportunity for each college to offer what its community needs without being shackled by its poverty. On the other hand, the provision of a set amount per FTE student as the foundation for all will have the effect of nudging the colleges toward uniformity. Like all of the plans except the market-economy plans, this one does not help the private sector (criterion four).

The foundation plan would appear at first glance to meet well the fifth criterion, that of protecting the public purse. The amount to be raised by the required local tax rate (and tuition if charged) and the number of FTE students can be estimated, and from this the amount that will be required from the state treasury can be estimated. But there is an insidious thing operating here, for there is a strong incentive to increase the number of FTE students. Let us suppose that there is no tuition, that there are 1,000 students, that the required local tax levy raises $500,000, and that the state foundation guarantee is $700 per student. Then the total amount of the foundation guarantee would be $700 times 1,000, which equals $700,000. Of this, the local district has raised $500,000 and the state must contribute $200,000. But now let the college manage to double the number of students it has, to 2,000. The total guarantee by the state would then be $700 times 2,000, which equals $1,400,000. But the required local tax rate still raises exactly as many dollars as before, $500,000. The state must now contribute $900,000. And so, at least up to the amount of the foundation guarantee, additional students are fully funded by the state with no additional local funding effort required, which represents a powerful incentive to increase enrollment, particularly in low-cost programs. (Since elementary and secondary schools cannot easily encourage additional enrollment, this is no problem with them.)

The foundation-plan model does little or nothing to prevent wasteful duplication among institutions or levels of education, and thus fails to meet the sixth criterion. The existence of local controls is the only feature of this plan that makes it better at meeting criterion seven, that of intra-institutional efficiency, than the planned-economy models (which fail miserably). The fixed local tax rate makes it poorer than the other mixed models.

If the foundation guarantee is set at such a level that the college with the greatest local taxing ability does not raise as much as the guarantee through the required tax rate and tuition, and if no college is allowed to raise additional money above the required amount through local taxes, the foundation program will be absolutely equalizing in the *Serrano* sense (criteria eight and nine). But these are two big ifs. Often the legislature, because of the pressure of other demands on the state treasury, sets the foundation guarantee unrealistically low, which means that the richest colleges will raise more money through the required tax rate and tuition, even with no state aid, than the poorer colleges will get with state aid. (This is usually compounded by the provision of a minimum flat grant which the richer colleges will receive even if they do not qualify for state aid under the foundation program.) In addition, because the foundation guarantee is set too low to provide an adequate program, the colleges are allowed to tax at a rate above the required rate, and these taxes are not equalized at all. The richer colleges, with the same tax effort, have more money to spend. However, we are discussing the models in their pure forms, and in its pure form the foundation plan is highly equalizing.

Power Equalizing

Of the models discussed in this chapter, this is the only community college financing system that is not currently used in some form in the United States. It has been chosen for discussion because it has been put forth by Coons, Clune, and Sugarman, who were responsible for much of the intellectual input to the *Serrano* and *Rodriguez* cases.[1] Power-equalizing has also been favorably adopted in various forms by a number of states for financing elementary and secondary schools, but has not been widely discussed as a model for community college finance. The idea of the power-equalizing model is to allow the local entities controlling community colleges to decide, in cooperation with their communities, how much effort they wish to put into community college education while still not allowing differences in local taxable wealth to influence the amount spent. In the percentage-matching and flat-grant models, if the locality is allowed to tax without restriction, a district rich in tax wealth can raise a great deal more per FTE student than can a district poor in tax wealth making the same tax effort (in terms of the tax rate). Freedom to decide on local effort is preserved, but at the expense of allowing continuation of inequalities (the percentage-matching scheme actually exacerbates the inequalities). The foundation plan is an equalization plan, and if it is used in its pure form it achieves complete equalization by forcing all districts to tax at the same rate and insuring them all the same amount of money per student. It thus achieves equalization at the expense of forcing all districts into the same expenditure rate, even though some communities might have greater aspirations for education than others, and be willing to tax themselves more heavily for it.

The power-equalizing plan has also been described as a "guaranteed assessed valuation" or "guaranteed yield" plan. Essentially, each district is to proceed to raise money by levying a tax rate dependent only upon the amount of money per student it wishes to raise. For example, the state could guarantee that a district would have $300 per FTE student for each mill it decided to levy. Thus, a district levying a tax of four mills would have $1,200 per FTE student to spend. The district would levy this tax rate on the actual assessed valuation of property in its district. If it raised less than $1,200 per student, the state would supply the rest. If it raised more than $1,200 per student, it would have to remit the extra to the state. The richest district and the poorest district would thus raise the same amount of money per student for the same tax effort.

The result of this scheme is similar to the percentage-equalizing plan used in New York's elementary and secondary schools (not to be confused with the percentage-matching plan used for New York's community colleges). An important difference is that the power-equalizing method is susceptible to variations that could be used by the state to nudge districts in a direction it thought desirable without putting them in a strait-jacket. For example, suppose a state decided that an expenditure of around $1,200 per FTE was desirable, and that a tax levy of four mills was an appropriate level. It could set up the following power-equalized schedule:

Tax rate	Dollars per student guaranteed
1 mill	$ 200
2 mills	400
3 mills	800
4 mills	1,200
5 mills	1,300
6 mills	1,400
7 mills or more	1,500

Districts could then levy any tax rate they wished, and any two districts levying the same tax rate would receive the same number of dollars per FTE student. It would be obvious to all that levying the third and fourth mills would bring them twice as much money per student as did the first and second mills, but that from the fifth mill on diminishing returns are received, and there is no increase at all in income from levying more than seven mills. Most districts would tend to levy around four mills.

There has been a great deal of favorable discussion of power equalizing at the elementary and secondary level, but this new concept took time to take hold. In 1969 only seven states had systems partially based on this concept. However, as of late 1975 twenty-one states distributed part of the elementary and secondary funds on a power-equalizing basis. But no state uses this method to finance its community colleges.

The power-equalizing plan would probably be similar to the foundation model with regard to the first criterion of serving those otherwise not well served. It suffers from the same problem as the flat-grant and foundation programs with regard to the second criterion: the use of FTE students as the measurement of financial need may tend to discourage the offering of nontraditional educational opportunities for fear that they would not be adequately recognized in the formula. On the other hand, power equalizing does respond to community needs, for it is specifically designed to allow the local community to decide upon and meet its own needs without being shackled by its poverty. As with all the planned-economy and mixed models, this one does nothing to help privately supported education, criterion four.

Unfortunately, like the percentage-matching plan, the power-equalizing plan has a major flaw when it comes to the fifth criterion, keeping expansion within bounds. Because local districts are allowed to decide upon the amount of their levies, the amount that must be supplied by the state treasury cannot be easily predicted, nor can it be easily limited without destroying the equalizing aspects of the scheme. State officials tend to fear that this plan would encourage poor districts to levy high tax rates knowing that for every dollar raised locally several dollars would come from the state. At the same time, the rich districts might decide to limit their spending, thus returning very little money to the state. Actually, this eventuality seems unlikely, because rich areas typically have higher aspirations, and would be unwilling to put up with the limited expenditure per student guaranteed by a low tax rate.

The power-equalizing plan also suffers from a flaw of the foundation plan, in that colleges are encouraged to expand enrollments with the knowledge that additional students would, in effect, be fully paid for by the state. Because it encourages districts to work out their own programs, this plan does nothing to prevent wasteful duplication among and within the levels of education, which is criterion six. On the other hand, it is similar to percentage matching in doing a better than average job of promoting efficiency within a local college.

Used in its pure form, the power-equalizing plan should meet completely criteria eight and nine, that of equity to student, in the *Serrano* sense, and to the taxpayer, the latter because it allows local communities freedom of choice as to the tax effort to be made for community colleges. Both the power-equalizing and the foundation-program models theoretically should provide more equity to students across a state than do either the flat-grant or percentage-matching models. That is, a given amount of state money can achieve more equity for students under an equalization program than could the same amount of money under a flat-grant program. Equity in a flat-grant program increases as the grant becomes a larger percentage of the cost of education. The kind of equity guaranteed by an equalization program could occur with the flat grant only if the grant were 100 percent of cost. This would be very expensive for the state, for there would be no local contribution.

Summary

The models discussed in this and the previous chapter, plus the two modified models to be discussed in the next chapter, and the way they meet the criteria of chapter two, are summarized in Table VII (page 72). It is interesting to note that the models in actual use in the United States at the present time, which are all planned-economy and mixed models, appear to meet the criteria less well than do any of the market models. Yet it seems unlikely, from a political viewpoint, that the state systems of community colleges that have been built up with public money, and in which people now have a vested interest, will be allowed to become private institutions. It therefore behooves us to ask whether there are improvements that could be made on any of the planned-economy or mixed models that would improve the way in which it meets the criteria. This possibility is discussed in chapter six.

Federal Aid to Community Colleges

Federal aid, which constitutes only about eight percent of the income of community colleges and seems unlikely to increase in the near future, has not been considered here for a variety of reasons.

TABLE VII:

How the Models Meet the Criteria

Model	Criterion Number								
	1	2	3	4	5	6	7	8	9
Market Economy Models									
Completely Private	-	++	-	++	++	+	++	--	++
Private with Student Grants	+	++	-	++	-	+	++	-	++
Private with Institutional Grants	-	++	-	++	-	+	+	-	++
Planned Economy Models									
Centralized Control	+	--	--	--	++	++	--	++	++
Decentralized Control	+	-	-	--	+	+	--	++	++
Modified Decentralized Control	++	-	+	+	+	+	--	++	++
Mixed Models									
Percentage Matching	-	++	++	--	--	--	+	--	--
Flat Grant	+	+	+	--	-	--	+	-	-
Foundation Plan	+	+	+	--	--	--	-	+	+
Power Equalizing	+	+	++	--	--	--	+	++	++
Modified Power Equalizing	++	++	++	+	+	--	+	+	+

Key: + + Meets the criterion very well   + Meets the criterion less well
         -- Meets the criterion very poorly   - Meets the criterion poorly

Short definition of criteria

1 Serves those not otherwise well served
2 Provides programs not otherwise provided
3 Responds to community needs
4 Helps preserve the private sector
5 Keeps expansion within bounds
6 Inter-institutional efficiency
7 Intra-institutional efficiency
8 Equity to students
9 Equity to taxpayers

The U.S. Constitution does not mention education and thus reserves it as a power delegated to the states and their citizens; however, the constitution of every state specifically mentions the state's responsibility in the field of education. To the extent that education is a local rather than a state function, it is so because the state has delegated certain powers and responsibilities to local bodies. But these local bodies are creations of the state, and can be regulated, modified, or abolished by the state. Thus, the major responsibility for financing public education lies with the state.

There is a legitimate function for the federal government in education, but only to the extent that national interests transcend state interests. The problem, of course, is to know in what ways this happens. The Association of American Universities has argued that it is in the national interest to maintain a group of high quality research universities, and that only the federal government can be expected to provide the money in research grants that will maintain the health of these institutions. It should be no surprise that the Association of American Universities represents just such a group of universities.

The Carnegie Commission on Higher Education has argued for a program of institutional grants to colleges and universities, on the basis that this is what is needed to maintain the health of higher education in general in the United States. These institutional grants could be used by the institutions for any legitimate purpose, and the amount would be dependent upon degrees awarded, or some similar criterion.

Other groups have suggested other ways in which federal money should be used to promote higher education, but these two examples illustrate a point: the two main alternatives are to target the money on specific programs that are conceived to be in the national interest, such as particular research projects, or to grant general use money to the colleges and universities. Intuitively, it would seem that if there is a federal interest in education that is different from state interests, it rests in certain specific areas, and that the federal government could best use its money by targeting it to those areas that are agreed to be in the national interest, rather than the scattergun approach of general institutional grants.

What might these areas be? It seems probable that one of these areas is indeed research. Only the federal government can decide what the most appropriate priorities for research are. This is not to deny that states, particular universities, or specific individuals may have different priorities, and that these perhaps should be funded by someone. But the federal government is in the position to decide that a particular area requires a massive effort, be that area energy, environment, or space, and see to it that a large amount of money is funneled into those institutions, spread across many states, that are most qualified to engage in this research. In this area of research, it is clear that the money should be carefully targeted. A program of institutional grants, based on the number of students in the institution or some such criterion, would not be well spent. Some institutions would be starving for money for good research, while others were throwing it away on bad research. In addition, within institutions, there would be a tendency to spread the money rather evenly across departments, rather than awarding it to those departments most in need of research money. Fortunately, the federal government has realized that making grants to specific research projects, on the basis of an approved proposal, is the most efficient way of promoting research.

The other area in which the federal government has a legitimate interest is in promoting certain social and economic goals. Social goals currently looked upon favorably include promotion of educational opportunity for various minorities, and provision of equal opportunity for the poor. Economic goals include training of the skilled manpower needed for certain priority areas, such as those skilled in energy production and protection of the environment. It is not immediately as clear that these goals cannot be served through a program of institutional grants as is the case with research. The main problem of institutional grants is that they can have two opposite effects, neither of them good: if they are concentrated, they tend to go to those institutions that have the most prestige or that are the most sophisticated in working with the Washington bureaucracy; if they are, instead, spread around, they often tend to bolster ineffective and inefficient institutions. A better alternative would appear to be grants that are targeted to students, who may then use them at the institution of their choice. The grants would be used to promote federal priorities, with grants to poor and minority students to promote social goals, and grants to students enrolled in particular priority programs to promote economic goals.

A program of grants to students rather than one of grants to institutions is bound to be resisted by the institutions, but the combination of concentration on federal priorities while encouraging healthy competition among institutions appears the most reasonable course. Incidentally, such a course could be particularly helpful to the community colleges, which currently receive a rather small amount of federal aid (only about eight percent of their budgets in 1973). A priority program for the federal government would most certainly be to help provide better educational opportunity for the poor and racial minorities. Since these two groups are much more represented in community colleges than in other institutions, the community colleges would benefit proportionately more from such a program.

CHAPTER V

Tuition and Its Effects

PRIVATE institutions cannot of course compete on the same terms with public institutions that offer the same instruction, of the same quality, for a much lower price because of government subsidy. When faced with this kind of unequal competition private institutions often seek aid from both government and philanthropies or find some way to avoid direct competition.

The Private Sector

The private institutions, naturally, have sought to avoid the government control that often goes along with the subsidies they seek, for government control would make them like public institutions. So they seek subsidies with no strings attached, and have been rather successful doing this at the federal level (where most aid programs have made no distinction between private and public institutions except where religion is involved). The aid they have received has included grants for construction of facilities and contracts for training and research. Institutions have been willing to undertake the training and research contracts because there is no compulsion in taking them, and because the indirect cost recovery that is part of the contract is unrestricted money that the institution may spend as it wishes. In addition, they are often able to pay for part or all of the salaries of some faculty members who continue to render services to the college in addition to those they give under the terms of the contract. The insidious part of such contracts did not become apparent to most schools until the end of the 1960s when these institutions discovered that they had made commitments of space and personnel that they had planned to pay for with federal funds. When the federal government cut back on funding for these projects, many private schools found they had unnecessary staff and buildings that they had to continue to support. This helped to contribute to what Earl Cheit has called "the new depression in higher education."[1] State governments have also, in some cases, provided subsidies directly to private institutions. An example is the so-called "Bundy plan" in New York, which pays private institutions in the state a certain amount of money for each degree awarded.

In addition to these institutional subsidies, both federal and state governments have provided subsidies to students, either on the basis of academic merit or need, and students have been able to use these grants to enable them to attend either private or public institutions. It should be noted, though, that unless the grant to the student specifically involves a tuition waiver, rather than simply an amount of money, it does nothing to narrow the gap in tuition charges between public and private institutions.

In any case, government grants have helped some private institutions stay alive, but have done little to remedy the unequal competition of the public institutions. The data in Table II (page 19) show clearly that state and local money goes overwhelmingly to public institutions, and even the federal money goes in larger measure to public institutions. In addition, the four-year colleges and universities have been able to get a much greater share of the federal money than have the two-year colleges.

Private colleges and universities have also gone aggressively after private gifts and grants, and have done surprisingly well at it. In a period of rapidly rising expenditures for higher education, the contributions of private philanthropies as a percent of the budget have stayed about constant. It is difficult to know how much longer this can continue, and it is certain that college expenditures connected with raising this money have risen rapidly.

Here also, the private junior colleges are in a difficult position. Institutions attract gifts from alumni, friends, and foundations. But private junior colleges are less apt to have rich alumni, and many alumni who are rich went on to get a bachelor's degree at a four-year college to which they have transferred their allegiance. Foundations and friends tend to give money to those institutions that are prestigious. The private universities have usually been able to do rather well at this, but many four-year liberal arts colleges have had considerable difficulty attracting gifts, and private junior colleges have had even more difficulty. Unfortunately, this leads to a situation of "them as has, gits."

Private universities have not so far been forced to avoid direct competition with public universities. They have been able to offer the same courses (and of the same quality) as the public universities because the buying public believes the private university has something that the public one does not. Whether or not this is true is unimportant, so long as the students and their parents are convinced they are getting their money's worth from the higher tuition. This may be because of smaller classes, a better atmosphere, or a belief that the friends a student makes among high-income fellow students will be helpful to him later in life.

The private liberal arts colleges have become less able to exert the same sort of attraction, and many of them faced tremendous difficulties as they found themselves unable to compete with the state colleges. The schools that have managed to compete successfully have done so by offering special programs—European campuses, work-study programs, and the like.

The private junior colleges have been least able to compete on the basis of prestige, now that the day of the finishing school is over. Instead, they have had to develop specialized programs not offered elsewhere and cater to the small group of students who want such special programs. The result has been a great diversity among those private junior colleges that survive. But the public community colleges have not felt themselves bound by tradition, and have hastened to offer special programs whenever they detected the need. The result has been a difficult situation for private junior colleges.

It is clear that these alternatives for private higher education may have helped some, but probably not enough. Many private institutions are in serious financial trouble and a few have had to close their doors. And it is evident that at the bottom of the problem is unequal competition from low tuition public institutions. It is time to ask seriously whether this should be allowed to continue indefinitely.

Vocational Education

Another area of concern regarding tuition is its effect on the supply of trained manpower: are present methods of funding higher education alleviating or exacerbating national employment problems? and what is the community colleges' responsibility regarding vocational education? In a chapter entitled "The Vocational Education Dilemma" Edmund Gleazer points out that students tend to stay away from vocational programs:

> Educators and taxpayers have reason to be concerned about the discrepancy between the numbers of students expected to enroll in occupational programs and the smaller numbers who do. Why be concerned? Some reasons are obvious: skilled manpower may not be pre-

pared for society's complex tasks. And the tone of our national life could be affected negatively if large numbers of college graduates are unemployed or underemployed.[2]

The reasoning here illustrates the problem of public community colleges operating in a planned-economy mode to prepare students to operate in a market economy. Many countries with planned economies use the manpower planning approach to determine the amount and kinds of education to provide. But these countries tend also to assign people to jobs instead of letting them assign themselves through the operation of the marketplace. In our market economy, providing vocational education courses on the basis of projected manpower needs contributes to the dilemma, and low tuition exacerbates it. The main problem with vocational education is the low prestige associated with it. If the market were allowed to operate as the market economists envision it, this low prestige would reduce the supply of trained personnel. The shortage would elevate their wages until the extra pay overcame, for a sufficient number of people, the low prestige of the job. By providing industry with a plentiful supply of trained manpower, and at a low cost to those trained, which is often the case today, community colleges are enabling industry to pay lower wages for those jobs than they would otherwise have to, which does nothing to counterbalance the low prestige of the jobs. For this reason, the provision of low-cost vocational education by the community colleges is open to serious question.

Public Institutions

It has long been a philosophical position of those connected with the community college movement that tuition should be either very low or nonexistent, in order to encourage access by those who have found access to traditional institutions difficult. It has been pointed out in an earlier section that this position has apparently not made much of an impact upon legislatures for, except in California, there are tuition charges in all states, and the income from tuition is at least as great a percentage of the budget for public community colleges as it is for public four-year institutions.

An estimate of actual levels of tuition was obtained from the questionnaire on public community colleges. Respondents were asked for an estimate of the average tuition and fees paid at community colleges in their state in 1972-73. Where these were expressed in terms other than a yearly amount, they were changed to an imputed yearly amount on the assumption of 30 semester hours or 45 quarter hours per year. The figures for the 36 states and Puerto Rico in the sample are given in Table VIII.

TABLE VIII:

Average Community College Tuition and Fees from 36 States and Puerto Rico, 1972-73

Tuition and Fees (Annual)	Residency of Student		
	In District	**In State**	**Out of State**
Mean of the Responses	$254	$356	$764
Range for Two-Thirds of the States	$153 to $359	$197 to $507	$464 to $1,076
Lowest Tuition	$0[a]	$0[a]	$71[b]
			$360[c]
Highest Tuition	$490[d]	$800[e]	$1,400[f]

[a] California   [d] New York
[b] Puerto Rico   [e] Arizona and Pennsylvania
[c] Georgia   [f] New Jersey

There are two other philosophical thrusts of community college supporters (in addition to their position on low tuition) that bear on this matter. One is the insistence on the importance of local decision-making, in order that the community college may truly reflect in its program the needs and desires of the community in which it is located. The other, perhaps not espoused by as many, is the position of the *Serrano* case, that local discrepancies in taxable wealth should not be allowed to influence the quality of the program offered by the community college.

These three philosophical positions tend to be in conflict with each other, a tendency that unfortunately has not been fully recognized by those who espouse them. Decision-making independence is highly dependent upon relative fiscal independence. But both equalization of local fiscal ability and reduction or abolition of tuition imply a greater financial commitment from the state. And it is foolish to think that control does not follow money. Those who provide money have a natural interest in seeing that it is wisely used. And those who appropriate public money have a responsibility to their constituents to exercise control over its expenditure. An instructive example may be the public schools, which in almost all states are controlled by local governing boards but receive large grants from the state for "unrestricted" use. A conversation with the superintendent or a knowledgeable board member of a school district will bring some idea of the great extent to which freedom of operation of the local school district has been proscribed by a thicket of state laws and regulations of the state board of education.

The surest way to retain freedom of action is to gain as much financial independence as possible. And the way for a public institution to do this is to have as many different sources of money as possible. The smaller the percentage of the budget being provided by one source, the less that source is apt to want or be able to dictate the college's decisions. The four most important sources of funds for public community colleges are the federal government, state government, local taxes or appropriations, and tuition. Of these, the amount from the federal government, although important, is not a large percentage of the budget and is not likely to increase. Community colleges should ask themselves whether they value the idea of free tuition sufficiently well to imperil their freedom of action. Since those who advocate low or no tuition do so because they believe it encourages wider access to higher education, we must next examine the effect of tuition on students.

Effect on Students

Some economists have questioned whether free tuition is effective in encouraging the attendance of low-income students. They have pointed out that, of the expenses connected with attending college, by far the largest (often larger than all of the other expenses put together) is the cost of foregone income. That is, while students are attending college full-time, they are unable to work full-time, and as a result do not obtain income they otherwise would have had. This is not of great importance to those whose family finances are adequate. But for many low-income people, a job is necessary for support. If students must give up earning an income necessary to their family in order to attend school, free or low tuition would not encourage them to do the latter.

Community colleges do have a much higher percentage of the poor, of minority group and older students than do the four-year institutions. But it is not clear that low tuition is a major reason for this. Perhaps proximity, evening classes, and encouragement of part-time study are much more important, for all of these make it possible for a student to pursue his or her studies without having to give up a job. Of course, for the person without a job, there is no cost of foregone earnings, and low tuition may be important to his school attendence. We do not know what percentage of students are in this category, although the data in Table IX (page 100) indicate that only about one-fourth of the students attending community colleges part-time in 1972 were unemployed or not in the labor force. Since so little is known about the independent effect of low or no tuition on the decision of various groups of students to attend community colleges, a rigid position on tuition may not be justified.

On the other hand, it is clear that, other things being equal, students who are not rich will probably be more apt to attend college if the tuition is low than if it is not, even though we don't know how great the effect is. But it is also clear that as family income increases, the deterrent effect of higher tuition diminishes. The result, then, is that charging low tuition to all students, rich and poor alike, is a very costly way of achieving the goal of helping needy students. It would seem much wiser to use the tool of low tuition selectively, either through tuitions scaled to ability to pay, or through grants to needy students. Through this method, aid can be targeted to where the college decides the need is, and at much lower cost to the supporting body of government than having low tuition for all.

There has been a great deal written about the form that student assistance should take.[3] The principal methods suggested have been tuition grants, ordinary loans, income-contingent loans, and work-study programs. Loans cost the government less, but the very people who are most in need of help are those least likely to take out the loans, for they fear the large long-term burden this puts on them and their families. The income-contingent loan idea[4] is not much more appealing than a conventional loan to those who shy away from loans. Jobs are unsatisfactory as a way of helping needy students for two reasons. One is that the time spent on the job takes away from study time, and this study time is often needed most by needy students. The other is that providing enough meaningful jobs is difficult and involves a good deal of administration. Often students are given "make-work" jobs they feel are demeaning, making them contemptuous of the whole process.

It does seem that students, no matter how poor, should make some contribution to their education, so that they have some stake in its outcome. An example is a proposal made several years ago by the Regents of the University of the State of New York.[5] They proposed that a system of grants be developed that would aid any student whose resources were below a certain point. The amount of aid would increase as the student's resources decreased, until a student with no resources at all would be eligible for aid up to the total amount of his expenses for tuition, books, and extra living costs (but not foregone income) with the exception of $400 per year that the student would have to provide.

There are problems involved in this approach. One of the biggest problems is that of properly defining and measuring the student's resources. Financial statements furnished by the student or his parents are difficult to verify for accuracy; an 18-year-old may declare himself independent of his parents and penniless only to collect student aid. But these are problems that can be solved. One group whose burden could be eased by this approach is that of the students from middle-income families who have suffered as tuitions have gone up and have found themselves ineligible for aid. By simply raising the qualifying income, these students could be helped. Of course, raising the qualifying income costs more money, but not as much as having low tuition for everyone, including the wealthy.

In summary, it is evident that the traditional cry for low tuition by those in the community college movement has not greatly impressed legislators, and may be doing the cause a disservice. Community college leaders should consider abandoning this position in favor of one that would provide a tuition at all public institutions, both two-year and four-year, that is more in line with the cost of instruction, with the provision that liberal student grants be made available on a basis that would encourage attendance by the poor and ethnic minorities. This position would have several good effects on community colleges. The first is that the increased tuitions would be very beneficial to the health of the private institutions. As was pointed out in the discussion of the criteria, it is in the interest of the public institutions to be concerned about the health of the private institutions. It is not necessary, however, to raise the tuition of public institutions to the level of private tuition. The prestige value of the private colleges, and their ability to specialize, would make it possible for them to compete effectively even though their tuitions were somewhat higher. A tuition of 50 percent of the cost of instruction at the public institutions might be a reasonable level.

A second beneficial effect is that the community colleges might, in effect, be able to have their cake and eat it too. To the extent that community colleges already have much larger proportions of needy students, those students would be eligible for grants that would lower the effective tuition to them, whereas this would not be as true for students in the four-year institutions. But the government money furnished in the form of grants to students would come to the community colleges indirectly in the form of tuition, rather than directly from the government, lessening or eliminating the ability of the government to dictate the use to which it could be put by the college.

A third beneficial effect is that with colleges charging a tuition closer to the actual cost of instruction, they would be able to offer types of courses that now arouse much community controversy. These tend to be in the area of avocational subjects, where the public quite rightly questions the use of public funds. Quieting the uproar about certain minor aspects of the curriculum could lead to a more reasoned discourse on what the overall offerings of the community colleges should be.

CHAPTER VI

Designing a Better System

T HE monetary value of a higher education as determined by economists should be interpreted with some caution, particularly by those concerned with community college education. Economists have not been very specific about the value of a community college education, partly because of the diversity of the programs offered by them and partly because of problems with analytical tools and data. In particular, one should question whether or not the seemingly small monetary returns for one to three years of college should be an indictment of the value of the community colleges.

Since it seems desirable to agree upon the value of something if we are to finance it publicly, and since the economists are of little help with the community colleges, the existence of these colleges has been justified on the basis that higher education in general has been shown to be of economic value, and the community colleges are equipped to furnish some unique services in higher education. These services are the education of those who find access to traditional institutions difficult; the offering of educational experiences not available in traditional institutions; and sensitivity and adaptability to the needs and desires of the community in which the college is located.

A set of nine criteria important in evaluating any plan for financing the community colleges were discussed in chapter two and then a number of models of community college finance were given and evaluated against the criteria. Federal financing and tuition were discussed separately from the models. In this summary the models will first be briefly recapitulated, then all of the models will be held up against each criterion. In other words, where before we looked at the models one at a time, we will now look at the criteria one at a time. Finally, some suggestions will be made for combinations of models that should do a better job of meeting the criteria than any single model previously discussed.

The first three models were grouped under the heading of market-economy models. In essence, they propose systems of higher education that are almost completely private, with only a minor amount of government financing, and little or no government control. The first model envisions a completely private system, with no government control of institutions, and no government financing, either of institutions or students. The second would relax these restrictions to the extent of allowing government grants to students, who would be free to use these grants in the institution of their choice. The third market-economy model would allow government financing of institutions on a formula basis, but with the institutions remaining private and the government money available for unrestricted use with no government controls.

Implicit in all three of the market-economy models is that colleges would charge a fee to students that approximates the cost of the service rendered, so that the marketplace could operate to furnish the education services that are wanted when and where they are wanted at the lowest possible total cost.

The next two models were based on the assumptions of a planned economy and represent the opposite extreme, that of complete governmental operation and the absence of any market mechanism for regulation. Implicit in these models is the replacement of the market mechanism with centralized planning as a way of regulating the kind and amount of educational services rendered. The first of these planned-economy models assumes complete centralization of financing and control. Allocations to colleges are made by the state on the basis of budgets approved by the state, and this right to approve the budget implies the right to control the activities of the institutions. The second assumes centralized financing (that is, there is no local financial contribution) with some decentralization of control. This decentralization is accomplished by providing the state money on a formula basis, so that the central approval of budgets is eliminated.

The last four models were termed mixed models. They incorporate some features of both the market-economy and the planned-economy models with some other features that are unique. All of them envision financial contributions from both the state and the locality. Thus, these models describe public colleges, as do the planned-economy models, while the market-economy models describe private colleges.

The first of the mixed models is based on the percentage-matching method of providing money to the local college from the state. The local college decides upon its budget, and the state simply agrees to provide a certain percentage of that budget. The second is the flat-grant model, where the state provides a certain amount of money per FTE (or on some other formula basis), with the rest being raised locally or through tuition. This is the second planned-economy model, but with the addition of a local contribution. The third mixed model is called the foundation plan. Here, the state sets a given amount per FTE student as the foundation guarantee. The college levies a stipulated local tax (and may or may not charge tuition). The state provides the difference between the amount of the foundation guarantee and what is raised through tuition and local taxes.

The last mixed model discussed is called power equalizing. Under this plan, the state would guarantee an assessed valuation per student, to free each community to set its own tax rate, but all communities that levy a tax at the same rate would have the same amount per student to spend. Those communities that raise less than this amount in local taxes would receive the difference from the state; those that raise more than this amount would have to remit the excess to the state.

Examples of all but one of the models currently exist in the United States; there is no state where the power-equalizing model is in use to finance community colleges.

Tuition is a necessary part of all the market-economy models, for it is the mechanism by which supply and demand are regulated. Tuition is not a necessary part of the other six models, but neither is its use proscribed by any of them. Tuition is important for its effects on private institutions, on public institutions, on the supply of trained manpower, and on students. Low tuition in the public institutions subjects private institutions to unfair competition, which must be alleviated in some way if the private institutions are to survive. The best way to alleviate the unfair competition would be to raise the level of public tuition. Low tuition in the public institutions adversely affects their autonomy. The more diverse the sources of funding of the public community colleges, the more freedom they would have from outside influence, and therefore more opportunity to meet local needs. Low tuition in vocational programs, and the provision of programs to satisfy projected manpower needs rather than student demands, exacerbates the problem of low prestige attached to vocational programs. High tuition in the public institutions makes attendance by the poor more difficult, but government grants to poor students are a much less expensive way of remedying this than providing low tuition to rich and poor alike.

Federal involvement was discussed separately, and government grants to students were favored as the main or only method of federal financing of higher education. This method decreases federal interference with institutions while allowing the government to target its aid to students in such a way as to meet national priorities. And it avoids excessive subsidization of inefficient and ineffective institutions.

Meeting the Evaluation Criteria

Some of these models meet the criteria given for judging community college financing plans better than do others.

The *first criterion* was that the method of financing the community colleges should enhance, rather than impede, the ability of the community college to serve those who find access to traditional institutions difficult: the poor, ethnic minorities, those past the usual college age, those with full-time jobs, those whose past academic record was mediocre. The market-economy models of finance would tend to impede the ability of the community colleges to serve the poor, for the essence of the market model is to charge a price that reflects the cost of furnishing the service. Any system of financing that charges tuition will of course make it more difficult for the poor to attend unless special provisions are made. But it is much less expensive for the public to subsidize poor students with grants than it is to provide low or no tuition for rich and poor alike, and receiving a substantial proportion of its money from tuition has important other advantages for the community college.

Tuition is not an important deterrent for those other than the poor who find access to traditional institutions difficult. The community colleges have served them by their open admission policies, by being in the community instead of some distance away, and by offering courses after working hours and encouraging part-time study. Private institutions might be even more ready to adapt themselves in this way than public institutions. Thus a completely private system and a private system with grants to institutions meet the criterion in a mixed way, with private adaptability working favorably for all but the poor, and tuition working against the poor. A private system with grants to students, if it incorporates student aid on the basis of financial need, eliminates this discrimination against the poor, and the model would then meet the first criterion well.

Because meeting the first criterion is mainly a function of tuition (for the poor) and of the ability to offer a variety of programs, the planned-economy and mixed models differ in the way they meet criterion one. Since tuition is neither prescribed nor precluded by these models, the extent to which tuition is not offset by grants to needy students will limit meeting their needs. For these and other groups that find access difficult, the ability to serve them is also limited by the ability to finance an adequate program. This is generally good in the planned-economy models, poor in the percentage-matching model, somewhat better in the flat-grant model, and good in the foundation and power-equalizing models.

The *second criterion* was that the finance method should enchance the ability of the college to provide courses and programs not provided, or insufficiently provided, by traditional institutions. The market-economy models are eminently suited to this criterion, for private enterprise is quick to find those things for which the demand is greater than the supply (of for which there is a potential demand that can be stimulated), and quick to meet the demand. Private institutions would have few or no government restrictions to keep them from offering these nontraditional educational experiences.

The planned-economy models suffer from the problems of bureaucratic inertia, which tends to stifle innovation, and thus they are not able to offer many nontraditional programs. However, decentralized control, even under a planned-economy financing system, would enable an institution to meet the criterion better than would centralized control. The mixed models, though they would have less central bureaucracy to contend with, would still find offering innovative programs difficult because, for three of them, allocations from the state are based on formulas, usually involving the number of FTE students. If an innovative program has costs that are not accurately reflected in the FTE it generates, it would be discouraged by an automatic lack of funding. Only the percentage-matching model does not suffer from this deficiency, because the formula used is that the state pays a percentage of the budget.

The *third criterion*, that the finance program should enhance the ability of the college to respond to the particular needs of the community it serves, as that community sees its needs, is one of the most important. To the extent that those in the community who have the educational needs are able to pay for them, the market-economy models serve this criterion well: free of government interference, the colleges can offer whatever their clientele wants. However, with a private system these wants are made known only through the market. There is no way for the community, through its elected representatives, to express the general needs of the community, rather than simply the needs of those with economic power. So the market-economy models meet this criterion only to the extent that all are enabled to participate without regard to financial ability. The completely private model is poor in this respect, the private model with institutional grants only somewhat better.

The planned-economy models do not meet this criterion well either because of the central planning and control inherent in them.

A decentralized system would of course meet community needs better than a system under centralized control, but without a local financial commitment to the college, local decision-making is inhibited.

The mixed models all incorporate a substantial amount of local control and local financial involvement, and therefore are best able to respond to community needs. Percentage-matching and power-equalizing systems, in which the amount of state aid is conditioned by the local effort, do this better than do the flat-grant or foundation-plan models.

The *fourth criterion* is that of helping to preserve the health and independence of the private sector of higher education. In the pure form in which they have been stated, all the market-economy models satisfy this criterion, and none of the planned-economy or mixed models do. However, the provision of tuition in the public institutions at a rate not too far below that of the private institutions would do much to eliminate this failing in the planned-economy and mixed models.

The *fifth criterion* is that the finance plan should help to keep the expansion of the community colleges within the bounds of public willingness to support them, and should take into account the financial health of state and local governments and the competing demands on them for money. The completely private model meets this criterion well, because the price mechanism will automatically insure that the offerings will be suited to the public's willingness to pay, and there is no governmental support. The private system with student grants or with institutional grants meets the criterion less well, because any grants have an effect on the price mechanism, and because the colleges, by expanding, can put increased demands on the public treasury. However, because the government commitment is smaller than in the mixed models (where the same unregulated demands can occur), these models do not pose as much of a danger to the public treasury.

Of the two planned-economy models, the first, that of centralized control, meets the fifth criterion well because the amount to be spent on the community colleges is directly determined by the political process at the state level. The decentralized-control model does not meet the criterion as well because the formula method of allocation allows colleges to expand and claim more from the state treasury than might have been planned for. However, the fact that the state controls the colleges enables it to put a brake on this tendency. Thus, both of the planned-economy models meet the criterion well.

The flat-grant and foundation-plan models force the state to contend with the possibility of increasing enrollments but without centralized control to keep it in check. The result is that if colleges expand their enrollments faster than the state is prepared to support them, the state may have to lower the amount of the flat-grant or the foundation guarantee. The foundation-plan and power-equalizing models have the additional flaw that when a college expands enrollment there is no need to increase local taxes. Under these models the state, in effect, pays the entire cost of additional students. The percentage-matching and power-equalizing models are similar in the lack of control the state has on their demands on its treasury. Not only is there no check on the expansion of the number of students, but there is no check on expenditure per student. Only if the state can have great confidence that the communities will be reasonable in their demands on its treasury can it use these models in their pure form. It is worth noting that with percentage-matching the state is worried about expansion of the budgets of the colleges in wealthy communities; with power-equalizing it is worried about budget expansion in poor communities. Because under both percentage-matching and power-equalizing the state is subject to open-ended demands on its treasury, it is usually necessary to control them in a way that has the effect of subverting these models and making them into flat-grant models. If the power-equalizing model were implemented anywhere in its pure form it would soon be found necessary to put similar controls on it.

None of the models would pose problems with local tax demands as they might with demands on the state treasury. In the market-economy and planned-economy models there are no such demands; in the mixed models the decision on the amount of local taxes is made by elected representatives of the taxpayers.

The *sixth criterion* is that the finance program should help to prevent wasteful duplication among institutions and among the levels of education. Whether or not the market-economy models do this is a matter of definition or ideological positon. Those who favor the market models point out that although there are no government controls to prevent duplication in these models, and that there is apt to be duplication wherever an institution feels it can sell a program, the market mechanism automatically prevents wasteful duplication. Those who are opposed to the market model feel that competition, which encourages investment in programs and facilities that may not turn out to be economically viable, and thus abandoned, is inherently inefficient, and they therefore opt for planning instead. Whether the market models meet this criterion thus depends on one's outlook. In Table VII they have tentatively been assigned a "plus."

The planned-economy models are well suited to meet this criterion (with centralized control doing it better than decentralized control) because the planning inherent in them is designed to prevent wasteful duplication. On the other hand, the mixed models, emphasizing local decision-making, do not meet this criterion well at all.

The *seventh criterion* is that the finance program should encourage each college to operate its program efficiently. The profit motive inherent in the market models suits them to do this although they can be criticized for using the wrong criterion—profit—as a goad to efficiency. A private system with institutional grants doesn't do as well here as would the completely private system or the private system with grants to students because the institutional grants are not conditioned on efficient operation, and so tend to mute the operation of the market in promoting efficiency. The planned-economy models, on the other hand, do not meet this criterion, for the planning and directing efforts of a bureaucracy are poor substitutes for the market mechanism in promoting efficiency. The mixed models share this deficiency with the planned-economy models, but not to as great an extent. The local control inherent in the mixed models will tend to promote efficiency to some extent. In addition, where there is the opportunity for local decision-making on the tax rate (all mixed models except the foundation-plan) there will be a further incentive toward efficiency.

Although the *eighth and ninth criteria* are stated separately, they are tied together by the financing system in all but the private models, and so will be discussed together here. The *Serrano* criterion is that the education provided a student should not depend upon the wealth of the community in which he happens to live. Thus, if colleges in two communities are supported at least partially by local taxes, and these taxes are not effectively equalized by the state, the students in the poor community will suffer if both communities are taxed at the same rate, or the taxpayers will suffer if both colleges spend at the same rate.

It might be thought that the market-economy models would fare well under these criteria, since there is no local tax contribution, and therefore spending presumably would not be tied to local ability. This is not true, however, for in a completely private system even a student able to pay the tuition would find that if he lived in a poor community the quality of the education he could purchase there would be poorer than that in more wealthy communities, for private institutions must gauge their offerings to the ability of most of their clients to pay. The other two market-economy models do better in this respect because the ability of colleges in poor areas to offer programs is enhanced by the grants to students or institutions. However, there is still a large dependence on local wealth. On the other hand, the lack of dependence on local taxation (the student or institutional grants come from statewide taxes) means that the ninth criterion is met very well.

With all of the planned-economy and mixed models, a failure in one criterion is a failure in the other, as stated above. The two planned-economy models meet the criteria because there is no dependence on local taxation and spending per student tends to be equalized across the state. Of the mixed models, percentage-matching meets the criteria most poorly. The state simply reinforces the inequalities that are already present, making it possible for poor communities to offer only an inferior program even at a higher tax rate. The flat grant is only a little better in this respect, since the grant is usually only a small part of the cost of education, leaving all the rest of the money to be raised by unequalized local taxation or tuition. The foundation plan is somewhat better than the flat grant, because the foundation is usually a much larger percentage of the cost of education. Power equalizing, implemented in its pure form, would result in complete equalization, thus satisfying both criteria very well.

Since it is clear that none of the models meets all of the criteria well, the problem is to devise a financing method that, through one of these models, meets the criteria better than any of the pure models. There is no single answer to this, and each state will have to consider the financing of its community colleges not only in the light of these criteria but also with past history and situations unique to the state in mind.

A Balance Between Public and Private Schools

The market-economy model of private schools with grants to individual students meets more of the criteria well than does any other model, and it is tempting to use it as the base for a composite model, which is what a number of economists have done. Many other people feel this is unrealistic because the states are not about to dismantle their present systems of public community colleges. Their investment in them is too large and the vested interests are too powerful.

On the other hand, it would be a serious mistake to force the private sector completely out of higher education. It is in the self-interest of the public sector to see that this does not happen. The private sector, with its greater freedom, can offer specialized courses, programs, and facilities that the community colleges would find it difficult to offer, relieving the pressure on the public community colleges to be all things to all people. The innovations pioneered by the private sector often help lead the way for the public sector.

The elimination of the private sector would also put an extra burden on the public sector. A mixed system of private and public education is much preferable to either system by itself. But if the private system is to be effective it must be economically viable. And this viability is being seriously threatened by the competition of low-tuition public higher education. The same increase over time in unit costs that results from a labor-intensive operation afflicts both private and public colleges, and the private colleges have been forced into substantial increases in tuition to balance their budgets. Although public institutions, too, have been raising their tuitions, the dollar gap between private and public tuitions continues to increase each year, putting an ever greater squeeze on the private institutions.

We can help to preserve the health of the private sector either by narrowing the tuition gap between private and public colleges or by institutional grants to private colleges. Of the two, the first is preferable by far. Institutional grants subject private institutions to public control, and also contribute to a decreased incentive to operate efficiently. Presently ineffective institutions may be aided while new and more effective institutions would find it difficult to qualify for aid. But narrowing the tuition gap will simply enable the private sector to compete on a fair basis, without exerting governmental control. Of course any increase in tuitions in the public sector must be accompanied by student aid for those who would be priced out of the market by the higher tuitions. This student aid should be provided by the federal government to such students and for such purposes as meet national priorities. States should supplement this aid at least to the extent of insuring that all students who desire a higher education are enabled to pursue it regardless of their financial ability. The model of student aid proposed several years ago by the New York Regents (discussed in chapter five) would best satisfy this demand.

To insure the health of the private sector it would not be necessary, or even desirable, to close the tuition gap completely, but only to narrow it substantially. And this is the only action that should be taken (aside from allowing students to use their grants in either a private or a public institution) if we are also to preserve the independence of the private sector.

Two Composite Models

This leaves the form of the finance program for the public sector to be considered. States may opt either for a system of public community colleges wholly financed by the state, or one in which local communities share in the financing. Of the two, the system with a local financial commitment should be preferred because the individual colleges in such a system will be better able to meet the needs and desires of their communities.

Given below are two composite models, one for states that choose a system without a local financial contribution, and one for states that want a state-local financial partnership.

Modified Decentralized System

For states that choose to have a system with no local financial contribution:

1. Tuition for in-state students should be set to furnish at least 50 percent of the current operating cost of the college. This is to prevent unfair competition with private institutions. This provision should apply to all public higher education in the state, not just to the community colleges.

2. There should be a system of student grants supported by state and/or federal money that would guarantee access to an education for any student no matter how poor. The grants could be used in public or private institutions in the state. The amount of the grant should depend upon the cost of education (including both tuition and living expenses) at the institution chosen by the students and be based upon their own financial need. The threshold of the grants should be set at such a level that middle-class students who find access difficult would also receive some help. Even the poorest students should be expected to provide a little of the cost themselves.

3. The state money going directly to the institutions should be allocated by the state on a formula basis (as in the planned-economy model with decentralized control), with minimal state control over local use of this money. The state may enforce general policy decisions about number of students, their qualifications, the educational programs to be offered, and so on. But it should avoid the detailed control implied in approval of a line-item budget with no opportunity to shift money among line items.

4. The formula should not be a simple one, granting simply a fixed number of dollars per FTE student, for this would discourage colleges from offering costly programs. Conversely, complicated formulas, such as are in use in North Carolina, are too cumbersome and the allowances are often unrealistic. The best compromise is probably to classify courses or programs into cost categories, with an allowance per FTE student for each based on cost studies. Five to 10

cost categories should be manageable. In addition, a small portion of the budget could be approved separately by the state on the basis of unique needs of particular colleges.

5. A governance mechanism should be developed that would maximize local decision-making and initiative within the constraints of state priorities, and would formalize an input from the community on what the program of the college should be.

The modified decentralized model is an improvement over the usual decentralized model in the way it meets the first, third, and fourth criteria. It meets the second and the fifth through ninth criteria in the same way that the regular decentralized model does. It meets the first criterion, that of access, better than does the decentralized model because the system of student grants that is part of it will insure access by those who otherwise might have financial difficulty. It should be better at meeting the third criterion, that of meeting community needs, because of the presumably improved governance mechanism which is hinted at (but not specified). The extent to which it is better at meeting this criterion depends on the success of such a governance system. Finally, this model is better at meeting the fourth criterion, of helping to preserve the private sector, because of the increased tuition of the public institution coupled with student grants to the poor that can be used in public or private institutions.

Modified Power-Equalizing System

For states that choose to have a state-local financial partnership:

1. Tuition should be charged, and a program of student grants set up as described in steps 1 and 2 (on the previous page) for the completely state-financed system.

2. The state-local partnership should be based on a power-equalizing model. Equity to the student and to the taxpayer demands either a foundation-plan model or a power-equalizing model if there is to be a state-local partnership. The power-equalizing model is preferred because it leaves to the local community the decision as to how heavily it should tax itself for community colleges while putting all communities on an equal footing with regard to the amount raised for a given tax effort.

3. In order to keep the finance plan from putting such a heavy and unpredictable burden on the state treasury, the power-equalizing model should be formulated in terms of a guaranteed assessed valuation *per capita* in the district rather than *per student* in the school. The original power-equalizing concept as put forth by Coons, Clune, and Sugarman was designed for elementary and secondary education, where attendance is nearly universal and there is no way for a school district to make unusual demands on the state treasury

by starting programs that attract more students. But when the plan is applied to community colleges this becomes a problem (it is also a problem for the other plans involving state-local sharing). In effect, under the power-equalizing plan as described earlier (where there was a guaranteed assessed valuation per student), if a college can attract additional students it will receive complete financing for them from the state. This puts a premium on college expansion that may not be in the state's interest.

On the other hand, by expressing the power-equalizing concept in per capita terms, colleges in different communities raise the same number of dollars per capita for the same tax effort, regardless of the actual local taxable wealth per capita. They can then choose to spend this money for community colleges in the way they see fit. In addition to reducing the temptation to raid the state treasury, this plan has the further advantage of untying the money received from the method of counting students. This would encourage the offering of innovative programs for which it is difficult to define FTE students.

An example will help this explanation. Suppose a community college district has a population of 100,000, and has a community college with 2,000 students. The conventional power-equalizing formula might guarantee a tax base of $150,000 per student. This would allow this community to provide an expenditure of $1,500 per student at a tax rate of 10 mills.*

Suppose the district had an actual assessed valuation of $100,000,000. At the 10 mill rate it would raise $1,000,000, and the state would pay the district the difference of $2,000,000 between that and the guarantee. Now suppose the district were able to expand its enrollment to 4,000 students. Since the guarantee is on a per student basis, the district is guaranteed an assessed valuation of $150,000 x 4,000 = $600,000,000. A tax of 10 mills on this would guarantee $6,000,000, which is still $1,500 per student. But the actual assessed valuation of the district has still stayed the same, and with a 10 mill tax rate it only raises $1,000,000. The state must come up with $5,000,000. In other words, it has financed the entire cost of the additional students.

Alternatively, as is being proposed here, the state could guarantee a tax base of $3,000 per capita. Since there are 100,000 residents, this amounts to guaranteeing an assessed valuation of $300,000,000. A district tax of 10 mills would then guarantee raising $3,000,000, with $1,000,000 coming from local taxes and the rest from the state. But

---

*The district would have a guaranteed assessed valuation of $150,000 x 2,000 = $300,000,000. A tax rate of 10 mills ($0.01 per dollar of assessed valution) would guarantee $300,000,000 x .01 = $3,000,000. This amount, divided by 2000 students, is $1,500 per student.

this amount would not depend upon the number of students in the college. If the college had 2,000 students, it could spend $1,500 apiece at a 10 mill tax rate, but if it expanded to 4,000 students it would have only $750 per student. In order to finance this expansion it would have to cut back expenses or increase the tax rate. The plan has untied the financing from the number of students and has made it dependent only upon the population of the district. Implicit in this is an assumption that total population is a better measure of the actual need of a community for community college education than is the ability of college administrators to attract students. This is an arguable assumption, but it is the assumption that is used in most state and federal programs of aid for municipal services other than the public schools.

A more extended example of how this modified power-equalizing approach would work, with the addition of tuition, is given in Appendix Four.

4. The tax base on which the guarantee is made would be all taxable residential property in the community college district. The nonresidential property would be assessed centrally by the state and taxed at a uniform rate by the state. The amount thus raised would be used by the state to help in its program of power equalization. Separating residential valuation thus from other valuation would reduce the discrepancies among districts in assessed valuation per capita, making a program of power equalizing more feasible and less expensive.

It appears that this modified power-equalizing model would meet the criteria of a good finance plan better than any model previously discussed and would have only one deficiency. In criterion one, access, it would be an improvement over ordinary power equalizing because the program of student grants would allow increased access by the poor. It would be similar to ordinary power equalizing in its effects on access of other groups.

It is better able than most plans to provide programs not otherwise provided because of the lack of a tie of the finance program to the number of students served. This makes it possible to offer programs that might not qualify for state aid under programs that tie aid to FTE. Thus criterion two is met. The local control implied in this program, together with the freedom to decide how much to tax without being hampered by wealth restrictions, makes this program meet very well the third criterion, of responding to community needs, just as ordinary power equalizing does.

As with modified decentralized control, modified power equalizing meets well criterion four, preserving the private sector, because of the higher tuition combined with a system of student grants. Of course, it would not preserve the health of the private sector as well as the market-economy models, which were all private to begin with.

This plan is better than ordinary power equalizing at meeting criterion five, that of keeping expansion of the system within bounds, for additional students are not subsidized by the state. However, it is not as good as complete centralized control at this criterion because the district can increase its state aid by increasing its tax rate. The plan should be roughly the same as ordinary power equalizing in the way it meets the sixth and seventh criteria of inter- and intra-institutional efficiency. Its poor ability to promote inter-institutional efficiency is its major flaw.

The question of the extent to which this plan meets the eighth and ninth criteria of equity to students and taxpayers is a difficult one to answer. If the actual needs of the district for the educational services of a community college are proportional to its population, then it is indeed just as equitable as ordinary power equalizing. Unfortunately, we have no good way of measuring the actual needs. Some would say that every student who can be enticed to a community college demonstrates a need; others would say that enrollment is often generated through advertising and other means that do not represent genuine need at all. Nevertheless, it seems probable that actual need does differ among districts, at least to some extent, and to the extent it does, this plan would not adjust to those differences in need. Thus it is not as good as ordinary power equalizing in the way it meets these two criteria. In essence, we have traded off some power in meeting these two criteria in order to enable the plan to better meet criteria two and five.

In Closing

This book has described and evaluated a number of models of community college finance. These fall into the general categories of market-economy models (which envision systems of private colleges), planned-economy models (which are for state-financed and controlled public colleges), and mixed models (which are models of public institutions with a mixture of revenue from tuition, local taxes, and state aid, and with a large measure of local autonomy). While one of the market-economy models has a number of desirable features, it has not been recommended because it is politically unrealistic to think of dismantling our systems of public community colleges. A planned-economy model that has been modified to improve some undesirable features has been suggested for those states that prefer a state system of colleges, rather than a state-local system. For those who prefer a system of public colleges in which there is a partnership between locality and state, a model has been recommended that is substantially different from any that is currently in use. It is based on the concept of power equalizing in use for elementary-secondary education in a number of states, but modifies the power-equalizing concept in several important ways to make it particularly applicable to community colleges.

However, the most important part of this book is not the recommendation of two specific finance models. Rather, it is the approach to making the recommendations that is important. Nine criteria were stated, explained, and defended as being appropriate in judging community college finance programs. These criteria were then used to judge a number of different models. (See Table VII, page 72.) It is this self-conscious attempt to decide what is important to us and then to evaluate our schemes against these criteria that should characterize our efforts in the area of educational finance and in many other fields as well. It is all too seldom used, and this is particularly true in the field of finance, where expediency is more the rule than the exception.

Appendix One

*Characteristics of Students in
Community Colleges and Technical
Institutes*

Unfortunately, it is not possible to get comparative data on all kinds of students in community colleges, to compare with similar data on students in other kinds of institutions. The National Center for Educational Statistics did do a study of those engaged in adult education in the United States in May 1969 and May 1972. The results are unpublished, but some preliminary results for those attending two-year colleges or technical institutes are shown in Table IX. They are incomplete, and the data to compare them with those taking adult education in other institutions are lacking, but it is evident from the data that the two-year colleges are serving a very substantial number of part-time students, and that number is increasing rapidly. Their average age is 33, about 13 years older than the average college undergraduate. Previous educational level covers the complete span from less than eight years to college post-graduate, but most have graduated from high school but not college. Negroes are underrepresented in comparison to their proportion of the population. Those taking such courses cover the occupational spectrum but there seems to be little in the offerings of these institutions to appeal to farmers or salespeople.

TABLE IX:

Demographic Characteristics of Students Engaged in
Part-Time Study in Two-Year Colleges and Technical Institutes, May 1972*

	Percent of Sample
Age	
17-24	30.8
25-34	32.1
35-44	18.8
45-54	12.1
55-64	4.5
Over 65	1.7
Sex	
Male	49.4
Female	50.6
Race	
White	91.6
Black	7.8
Other	0.6
Occupation	
Professional and Technical	16.3
Farm Manager	1.2
Manager and Administrative	6.8
Sales Personnel	4.5
Clerical	16.7
Craftsmen	10.8
Operators	7.7
Service Workers	11.7
Unemployed or not in labor force	24.3
Level of Education	
0-8 years	2.1
9-11 years	7.0
High School Graduate	44.4
Some college	33.6
College graduate	9.0
Some graduate credit	3.9

*The population consists of individuals 17 years of age or older, taking one or more courses at a two-year college or technical institute, but not full-time students. The number of individuals sampled in May 1969 was 1,550,000; in May 1972, 2,561,000.

Source: Test runs by National Center for Educational Statistics from the 1972 Adult Education Participation Survey, based on the Current Population Survey of the U.S. Census Bureau, May 1969 and May 1972.

Appendix Two

Criteria Proposed by the National Commission on the Financing of Community Colleges

In 1973 the commission* issued a report called *Financing Postsecondary Education in the United States* which used various criteria to evaluate how well institutions for postsecondary education were meeting their established objectives. Some of their objectives, or criteria, were quite similar to those in this book, others were rather different. Some readers may find one or more of these objectives more appealing than the criteria used in this book. If so, it should not be difficult to hold them up to each of the models proposed in chapters three and four.

The objectives listed by the commission are as follows:

1. *Student access.* Each individual should be able to enroll in some form of postsecondary education appropriate to that person's needs, capability, and motivation.

2. *Student choice.* Each individual should have a reasonable choice among those institutions of postsecondary education that have accepted him or her for admission.

3. *Student opportunity.* Postsecondary education should make available academic assistance and counseling that will enable each individual, according to his or her needs, capability, and motivation, to achieve his or her educational objectives.

4. *Educational diversity.* Postsecondary education should offer programs of formal instruction and other learning opportunities and engage in research and public service of sufficient diversity to be responsive to the changing needs of individuals and society.

5. *Institutional excellence.* Postsecondary education should strive for excellence in all instruction and other learning opportunities, and in research and public service.

6. *Institutional independence.* Institutions of postsecondary education should have sufficient freedom and flexibility to maintain

---

*Established by act of Congress under Public Law 92-318.

institutional and professional integrity and to meet creatively and responsively their educational goals.

7. *Institutional accountability.* Institutions of postsecondary education should use financial and other resources efficiently and effectively and employ procedures that enable those who provide the resources to determine whether those resources are being used to achieve desired outcomes.

8. *Adequate financial support.* Adequate financial resources should be provided for the accomplishment of these objectives. This is a responsibility that should be shared by public and private sources, including federal, state, and local government, students and their families, and other concerned organizations and individuals.

Appendix Three

*Description of State Finance Systems
for Community Colleges in 1973*

I. Planned-Economy Type with Centralized Control

Alaska and *Georgia* handle distribution in a similar manner: a legislative lump-sum appropriation is allocated by the regents on the basis of approved budgets. There is no local taxation.

Iowa has a local tax of three-quarters mill, which is essentially a state property tax for community college support. The allocation of state money is based on each college's budget for the previous year, plus an allowance for inflation, less tax revenue, tuition, and federal money.

In *Kentucky*, there is no money from local sources and the allocation to each community college is based on program need justification with priorities being set at both college and system level.

In *Massachusetts* the 16 community colleges are operated by the state with no money from local taxation or appropriation. Student tuition does not stay with the local college, but goes into the state general fund. While personnel are allocated among the colleges on something like a formula basis, the rest of the budget is not formula based. Colleges inflate their budget requests with the expectation that they will be cut by the state.

In *Montana* the legislature appropriates the money necessary to fund the budget approved by the state board of regents. This money is the amount of the budget less the tuition charged and the income from a mandatory local tax of three mills. This system does not fit as well into this model as do some others because there is a locally elected board of trustees for each college. The local three-mill tax, because it is mandatory, is really the equivalent of a state tax, rather than a local financial contribution. In any case, the state retains the power to approve the budget, and this implies the power to determine the program.

103

In *Oklahoma,* the method of allocation for the eight state-operated community colleges is the same as that for the rest of public higher education. Each college makes a budget request for more than it received the previous year. Each college gets what it received before plus a proportional share of the "new" money appropriated, which is usually less than the "new" money it requested.

Rhode Island has only one public community college, which is financed by the state through direct legislative appropriation.

The five community colleges in *Utah* are financed by a direct appropriation to each institution by the legislature, based on a budget developed by the State Board of Higher Education.

In *Virginia,* appropriations are made to the 21 community colleges on an individual basis by the state budget office, with each college treated as a separate state agency.

The four community colleges in *Puerto Rico* are branch campuses of the University of Puerto Rico, and are funded by direct legislative appropriation.

II. Planned-Economy with Some Decentralization

It is possible that the *Connecticut* system should be placed under the completely centralized model, since the state allocation is on a budget approval basis. But about 75 percent of the money is allocated through formulas derived from the number of FTE. Only about 25 percent is allocated on the basis of unique needs. There is no local contribution.

In *Florida* courses are costed in four groups, ranging from least to most costly, and the cost factors assigned range from 0.8 to 1.7. The number of FTE in each cost category at a college is multiplied by the base allowance per FTE and by the cost factor for that category. The sum of these calculations for the four categories determines the state allocation. Colleges with fewer than 1,300 FTE are allowed somewhat higher cost factors.

In *North Carolina* the state allocation is based on a detailed formula budgeting system, with a formula for practically every line item in the budget. Examples are one teacher per 22 FTE, with a flat dollar allowance per teacher, $2.50 per FTE for postage and telegraph in the administrative office; and a flat $400 for travel by the business manager. There is provision for local tax effort in North Carolina, which keeps its system from fitting this model completely. But only about 11 percent of the operating income was from local sources in 1971-72, and 75 percent was from state sources.

In *South Carolina,* at the time of the survey, the number of teachers in each subject area was determined by the FTE in the subject area and a specified pupil-teacher ratio for that area. The number of teachers was multiplied by a state average teacher salary to get the "direct cost." All other budget allowances were specified as a percentage of direct cost. There was a local contribution, but it was only 10 percent of the budget, and the state contribution was 69 percent. Since this survey was made, South Carolina has changed to a system similar to Florida's.

The state allocations to *Tennessee's* 11 community colleges are based on the use of detailed formulas, some based on FTE, others on such things as the number of library books or the number of square feet of floor space. The same formulas are also used for the university and the state colleges. There is no local contribution.

Washington uses a budget model that develops an allowance for programs and the expense categories within them on the basis of formulas. There is no local contribution.

III. Percentage-Matching

In *Maryland* the state pays 50 percent of the operating budget. Tuition is limited to 22 percent or less of the budget; the county share is 28 percent or more. The maximum state contribution is $700 per FTE. Income from state sources in 1971-72 averaged $671 per FTE. Thus, it appears probable that many of the state's community colleges actually receive a flat grant of $700 per FTE.

In *Missouri* the form of the arrangement is that of percentage-matching, in which the state pays 50 percent of the budget. But this state share is subject to a minimum of $320 per FTE and to a maximum of $400 per FTE. Thus only those colleges that budget between $640 and $800 per FTE are subject to the percentage sharing feature. The rest receive a flat grant of either $320 or $400. The average income per FTE from state sources in 1971-72 was $322.

In *New Jersey,* the law provides for the state to pay 50 percent of the cost of operation, up to a maximum of $600 per student. Income from state sources in 1971-72 averaged $605 per FTE, indicating that most, or all, of the colleges receive a flat grant of $600 per FTE.

The form of the *New York* system is that of percentage-matching, on the Pennsylvania principle of one-third each from state, locality, and student, except in New York City. There the state share is 40%, the city's share 60%, and there is no tuition.* However, the limits on the state share are $621 per FTE in New York City and $518 per FTE in the rest of the state. The information furnished on total income from state sources and total FTE indicate that the colleges actually received an average of $640 per FTE in 1971-72. A reasonable

---

*Tuition was instituted in the fall of 1976.

inference from this is that most, if not all, of the community colleges in New York receive a flat grant of either $518 or $621 per FTE, with additional money coming from the state for special programs.

Pennsylvania has apparently the purest form of percentage-matching. According to the information furnished, exactly one-third of the income of the colleges comes from the state, one-third from localities, and one-third from student tuition, in spite of the fact that the state share is limited to $400 per FTE.

IV. Flat Grant

Arizona makes a flat grant per FTE of $680 for the first 1000 students in a college, and $440 per FTE for the excess over 1,000. There is an additional amount for vocational-technical students of $272 per FTE for the first 1,000, and $176 per FTE for the excess over 1,000. Finally, there is an allocation of $135 per FTE for capital outlay.

Colorado has 12 community colleges, six of which are operated by the state, and were discussed under Model 11A. The six operated by localities receive a flat grant of $575 per FTE for academic students and $1050 per FTE for occupational students.

Kansas community colleges receive $14 per credit hour from the state.

In *Mississippi* 6 percent of the state money is distributed in the form of a flat grant per college (equal dollars per college); 94% is in the form of a flat grant per full-time day academic Mississippi student. Based on data furnished, it appears that this latter flat grant is approximately $330 per FTE. It is clear from the basis of the flat grant that the state does not intend to aid vocational students or part-time students in the community colleges. The probable effect is to establish the community colleges as academic institutions and relegate vocational students to other institutions, perhaps area vocational education centers. If this is so, it is possible that an additional effect is to establish the community colleges as predominantly white, and the vocational centers as predominantly black.

New Mexico provides a flat grant of $325 per FTE.

North Dakota provides a flat grant of $200 per FTE. However, if the community college levies a local property tax of at least four mills the state will provide $350 per FTE.

Oregon provides a flat grant of $743 for the first 500 students, $614 for the next 400 students, and $560 for all additional students enrolled at the college.

Texas provides $640 per FTE for academic students. Colleges receive money for vocational students at varying rates per student contact hour, depending on the program. There are 28 programs, with rates per contact hour ranging from $0.46 for nurse's aide to $2.59 for career pilot. Assuming 16 weeks in a semester and 15 contact hours per FTE per semester (the same as for academic students), the vocational rates would provide $220.80 per FTE for nurse's aides, and $1243.20 per FTE for career pilots. The contact-hour rates are based on periodically updated cost studies.

Wisconsin provides a flat grant of 55 percent of the previous year's statewide operating cost per FTE. Because academic FTE is computed on the basis of 15 contact hours per week, and vocational FTE on the basis of 22.5 contact hours per week, the effect is that of having a flat grant for academic students that is higher than that for vocational students, a switch from the situation in the other states that differentiate between academic and vocational.

The *Illinois* formula is of the foundation type, but the amount of equalization provided is quite small, so the effect is that of a flat grant of $570 per FTE for vocational students and $495 per FTE for all others. Only seven of the 47 community colleges in Illinois receive "equalization" aid from the state to help compensate for differences in local financial ability, and less than three percent of the state money goes for equalization.

Maryland's aid formula is percentage sharing in form, but most of the colleges probably receive the maximum of $700 per FTE as a flat grant.

Michigan's aid formula is a foundation plan in form, but the amount of equalization provided is small, and the effect is that of a flat-grant formula. The amount of the flat grant varies with the program and with the student's classification as in-district or out-of-district. Community colleges operated by kindergarten through high school district boards receive a flat grant of $391 per in-district FTE for liberal arts and business courses, of $956 for vocational-technical courses, and of $1,463 for health courses. The amounts differ slightly for other kinds of community college districts.

The form of the *Missouri* aid formula is percentage-matching, but the effect is apparently that of a flat grant of $320 per FTE for most colleges.

The form of the *New Jersey* aid formula is percentage-matching also, but the effect is that of a flat grant of $600 per FTE for most colleges.

The form of the *New York* formula is also percentage-matching, but the effect is that of a flat grant of $621 per FTE to the community colleges in New York City and of $518 per FTE to the rest of the community colleges in the state.

V. Foundation Plan

California is important in community college finance simply because more money is spent on community colleges in California than in any other state. California uses average daily attendance (ADA) instead of FTE to measure number of students. The foundation guarantee is $679 per ADA for regular students regardless of program. The required local tax effort is $0.25 per $100 of assessed valuation (2.5 mills). There is no tuition. (The foundation guarantee and required tax rate are less for "defined adults," in general, those over 21 not attending full time.) There is a minimum flat grant of $125 per ADA regardless of local fiscal ability. Equalization of local ability is provided, then, for the range of expenditures between $125 and $679. There is no equalization provided below $125 or above $679 per ADA.

While the *Illinois* state aid program has a foundation feature in it, the amount of money provided under this feature is quite small, and only 7 of the 47 community colleges in Illinois receive any of it. Of the total amount of state operating aid, about $50 million is in the form of flat grants and only about $1 million for the foundation-type equalization.

The effect in *Michigan* is similar. The foundation guarantee varies from $1091 per FTE for liberal arts to $2,163 per FTE for health students. From this is deducted $310 per FTE for tuition and the amount raised by a local tax rate of one mill or $390 per FTE. This has the effect of a flat grant of from $391 per FTE for liberal arts to $1,463 for health, plus a small equalization amount that applies only to the poorest colleges.

The *Wyoming* foundation guarantee is $810 per FTE for academic students and $1,215 per FTE for vocational students (more in smaller colleges). From this is deducted $150 per FTE to represent tuition, and the return from a four-mill tax on a defined local tax base. Tuition and required taxes on the tax base as defined do not raise as much as the foundation guarantee, so every college receives some equalization aid. In addition, every college district must levy the four mills, and none may levy more than this amount. This would provide complete equalization if it were not for the fact that the tax base as defined for the purposes of the foundation program is not the tax base on which the tax is actually levied. Because of this, equalization is not complete, but without data on the individual colleges it is impossible to say how incomplete.

VI. Other Systems

There are two states in our sample whose plans do not appear to fit well into any of the models.

Arkansas had only two community colleges in 1972-73, and there was a direct appropriation to each based on a budget approval, which may to some extent have included knowledge of the amount that could be raised by local taxation. Local tax rates were limited to 10 mills. If the colleges both taxed at the limit, the tax could be thought of as a state tax, and the system of distribution would essentially be that of the completely centralized model. If they varied their tax rates, this would not fit well into any of the models.

Ohio determines an allocation of state money for each college on the basis of formulas in the same way as most states classified in the decentralized model, except that the allocation completely ignores the substantial amount raised in local taxes and the differing fiscal abilities of the community college districts.

Appendix Four

*Community College Financing Under
a Modified Power-Equalizing Plan*

Table X gives some examples of how this proposed modified power-equalizing program would work in practice. Case A is an example of a community college district rich in property wealth. The college's trustees have decided on a budget of $1,000,000 for the college. Tuition is expected to raise half of this, leaving $500,000 to be raised by taxes (state or local). Case B is a community college district poor in property wealth that has also decided on a budget of $1 million, with half to be raised through tuition. The assessed valuation of district A is $110 million of which $10 million is industrial, leaving $100 million available to be taxed locally. District B has only one-fifth this amount of wealth, with $20 million available to be taxed locally. Both districts have a population of 50,000, so that District A has an assessed valuation per capita of $2,000, while that of District B is only $400.

Under the power-equalizing program, the state has guaranteed each district an assessed valuation of $1,500 per capita. Multiplying this by the population gives a guaranteed assessed valuation of $75 million for each district. Based on this assessed valuation, the tax rate necessary to raise the $500,000 needed by each district would be 6.67 mills ($0.667 per $100, or $6.67 per $1,000). Based on the actual assessed valuation, this tax rate would raise $667,000 in District A and only $133,400 in District B. Under the power-equalizing plan, the state would require District A to remit $167,000 to the state, and would provide District B with $366,600 in state money. This would leave each district with $500,000 it needed to balance its budget, and each would have levied the same tax rate.

Cases C and D show the same two districts, but each has decided on a budget of $2 million with half of it raised by tuition. Following through the steps shows that each would have to levy the same tax rate to balance its budget, and that tax rate would be twice the tax rate necessary for a budget of $1 million. The richer district would remit twice as much to the state; the poorer district would receive twice as much from the state.

110

Case E is the same as Case C, except that the district has a much greater proportion of industry in its tax base. The implication is that the residential and commercial base per capita is less than for Case C, and this is shown by the fact that the assessed valuation per capita available for local taxation is only $1,000. The net result is that this district, like C and D, would have to levy a tax of 13.33 mills in order to balance its budget. But, unlike District C, it would receive money from the state instead of having to remit money to the state.

TABLE X:
*Financing with a Modified Power-Equalizing Plan**

	Case A	Case B	Case C	Case D	Case E
Budget	1,000	1,000	2,000	2,000	2,000
Tuition	500	500	1,000	1,000	1,000
Remaining Budget	500	500	1,000	1,000	1,000
Total assessed valuation	110,000	22,000	110,000	22,000	110,000
Nonresidential assessed valuation	10,000	2,000	10,000	2,000	60,000
Residential assessed valuation	100,000	20,000	100,000	20,000	50,000
Population	50	50	50	50	50
Assessed value per capita	2	0.4	2	0.4	1
Guaranteed assessed value per capita	1.5	1.5	1.5	1.5	1.5
Tax rate required (dollars per $1000 assessed value)	6.67	6.67	13.33	13.33	13.33
Taxes raised locally	667	133.4	1,333	267	667
Received from state	0	366.6	0	733	333
Remitted to state	167	0	333	0	0
Net available to balance budget	500	500	1,000	1,000	1,000

*Figures given in thousands of dollars, except for line given for required tax rate.

Notes

Notes to Chapter I

[1]Michael Brick, "The Development of Higher Education in the United States," in *The World Yearbook of Education, 1971-72* (London: Evans Brothers Limited, 1971), p. 46.

[2]Walter I. Garms, "The Prediction of State-Local Expenditures for Higher and Lower Education in the United States," in Robert D. Leiter, ed., *Costs and Benefits of Education* (Boston: Twayne Publishers, 1975).

[3]F. F. Harcleroad, H. B. Sagen, and C. T. Molen, Jr., *The Developing State Colleges and Universities* (Iowa City: The American College Testing Program, 1969), pp. 18-21.

[4]F. Rudolph, *The American College and University* (New York: Alfred A. Knopf, 1962), p. 252.

[5]R. Freeman Butts and Lawrence A. Cremin, *A History of Education in American Culture* (New York: Henry Holt & Co., 1963), p. 103.

[6]Charles S. Benson, *The Economics of Public Education* (Boston: Houghton Mifflin Co., 1961), p. 314.

[7]James W. Thornton, Jr., *The Community Junior College* (New York: John Wiley & Sons, 1966), p. 51.

[8]Leland L. Medsker, *The Junior College: Progress and Prospect* (New York: McGraw-Hill Book Co., 1960), p. 11.

[9]Kenneth A. Simon and W. Vance Grant, *Digest of Educational Statistics,* 1972 Edition (Washington, D.C.: U.S. Government Printing Office, 1973), Table No. 110.

[10]Thornton, *Community Junior College,* pp. 51-54.

[11]Leonard V. Koos, *The Junior-College Movement* (Boston: Ginn & Company, 1925).

[12]Walter C. Eells, *The Junior College* (Boston: Houghton Mifflin Co., 1931).

[13]Carl E. Seashore, *The Junior College Movement* (New York: Henry Holt & Co., 1940).

[14]J. P. Bogue, *The Community College* (New York: McGraw-Hill Book Co., 1950), p. 239.

[15]Medsker, *Junior College*.

[16]Ralph F. Fields, *The Community College Movement* (New York: McGraw-Hill Book Co., 1962).

[17]Edmund J. Gleazer, Jr., *This is the Community College* (Boston: Houghton Mifflin Co., 1968), p. 52.

[18]Christopher Jencks and David Riesman, *The Academic Revolution* (Garden City, N.Y.: Doubleday & Co., 1968), p. 257.

[19]Selma J. Mushkin and Eugene P. McLoone, *Higher Education in the 48 States: A Report to the Governors' Conference* (Chicago: Council of State Governments, 1952), pp. 13-14.

[20]H. K. Allen and Richard G. Axt, *State Public Finance and State Institutions of Higher Education in the United States* (New York: Columbia University Press, 1952), pp. 3-5.

[21]From the *Second Newman Report: National Policy and Higher Education,* Cambridge: M.I.T. Press, 1973).

[22]Earl F. Cheit, *The New Depression in Higher Education* (New York: McGraw-Hill Book Co., 1971), p. 10.

[23]Joint Economic Committee of the Congress, *The Economics and Financing of Higher Education in the United States* (Washington, D.C.: U.S. Government Printing Office, 1969), pp. 107-204.

[24]Alice M. Rivlin and Jeffrey H. Weiss, "Social Goals and Federal Support of Higher Education—The Implications of Various Strategies," in Joint Economic Committee, *Higher Education in the United States,* pp. 543-555.

[25]Benson, *Economics of Public Education,* p. 314.

[26]Ellwood P. Cubberley, *School Funds and Their Apportionment* (New York: Teachers College, Columbia University, 1906), p. 17.

[27]George D. Strayer and Robert M. Haig, *Financing of Education in the State of New York* (New York: Macmillan Co., 1923), pp. 173-174.

[28]Harlan Updegraff and Leroy A. King, *Survey of the Fiscal Policies of the State of Pennsylvania in the Field of Education* (Philadelphia: University of Pennsylvania, 1922), chap. 2.

[29]John E. Coons, William H. Clune, III, and Stephen D. Sugarman, *Private Wealth and Public Education* (Cambridge: Harvard University Press, The Belknap Press, 1970).

[30]Henry C. Morrison, *School Revenue* (Chicago: University of Chicago Press, 1930).

[31]*Serrano v. Priest,* 5 Cal. 3d 584, 487 P.2d 1241, 96 Cal. Rptr. 601 (1971).

[32]*Rodriguez v. San Antonio Independent School District,* 337 F.

Supp. 280 (W.D. Tex., 1971); *San Antonio Independent School District* v. *Rodriguez,* 411 U.S. 28.

[33]For example, *Robinson* v. *Cahill,* 62 N.J. 473, 303 A.2d 273 (1973), in New Jersey; *Hollins* v. *Shoftstall,* Civil No. C-253652 (Ariz. Super. Ct., June 1, 1972) in Arizona; and *Milliken* v. *Green,* 389 Mich. 1, 203 N.W.2d 459 (1972) in Michigan.

[34]James S. Coleman and others, *Equality of Educational Opportunity,* (Washington, D.C.: U.S. Government Printing Office, 1966).

[35]See, for example, Samuel Bowles and Henry M. Levin, "The Determinants of Scholastic Achievement—An Appraisal of Some Recent Evidence," *Journal of Human Resources,* vol. 3, no. 1 (Winter 1968), pp. 3-24.

[36]For example, Harvey A. Averch and others, *How Effective is Schooling? A Critical Review and Synthesis of Research Findings* (Santa Monica: RAND Corporation, 1972) and Christopher Jencks and others, *Inequality: A Reassessment of the Effect of Family and Schooling in America* (New York: Basic Books, 1972).

[37]For example, James W. Guthrie and others, *Schools and Inequality* (Cambridge: The M.I.T. Press, 1971) and Charles R. Link and Edward C. Ratledge, "Social Returns to Quantity and Quality of Education: A Further Statement," *Journal of Human Resources,* vol. X, no. 1 (Winter 1975), pp. 78-89.

Chapter II

[1]Gary S. Becker, *Human Capital* (New York: National Bureau of Economic Research, 1964), Chapters IV and V.

[2]Walter I. Garms, "A Benefit-Cost Analysis of the Upward Bound Program," *Journal of Human Resources,* vol. 6, no. 2 (Spring 1971), pp. 206-220.

[3]American Association of Junior Colleges, *1972 Junior College Directory,* (Washington, D.C.: By the Association, 1972), p. 5.

[4]Milton Friedman, *Capitalism and Freedom* (Chicago: University of Chicago Press, 1962), pp. 85-107. See also Harry W. Knight and David S. Mundel, "Report to the Subcommittee on Management and Financing of Colleges of Committee for Economic Development by the Task Force on Alternate Sources of College Funding," (Washington, D.C.: Committee for Economic Development, 1972); and Neil Singer and Paul Feldman, "Criteria for Public Investment in Higher Education," in Joint Economic Committee of the Congress, *The Economics and Financing of Higher Education in the United States.* (Washington, D.C.: U.S. Government Printing Office, 1969).

[5]Jerome Karabel, "Community Colleges and Social Stratification," *Harvard Educational Review,* Vol. 42 (November 1972), p. 543.

[6]Richard A. Easterlin, "Does Money Buy Happiness?" *The Public Interest,* No. 30 (Winter 1973), p. 4.

[7]Vincent Tinto, "Public Junior Colleges and the Substitution Effect in Higher Education," Paper presented at the Annual Meeting of the American Educational Research Association, Chicago, Ill., April 1974 (ERIC document ED 089 808).

[8]Ibid., p. 16

[9]*Serrano* v. *Priest,* 5 Cal. 3d 584, 481 P. 2d 1241, 96 Cal. Rptr. 601 (1971).

Chapter III

[1]Governor's Commission on Education, *A Forward Look: Final Report of the Governor's Commission on Education* (Madison, Wisconsin: By the Commission, 1970), p. 120ff.

Chapter IV

[1]John E. Coons, William H. Clune, and Stephen D. Sugarman, *Private Wealth and Public Education* (Cambridge: Harvard University Press, The Belknap Press, 1970).

Chapter V

[1]Earl F. Cheit, *The New Depression in Higher Education; A Study of Financial Conditions at 41 Colleges and Universities* (New York: McGraw-Hill Book Co., 1971).

[2]Edmund J. Gleazer, Jr., *Project Focus: A Forecast Study of Community Colleges* (New York: McGraw-Hill Book Co., 1973, p. 113.

[3]See, for example, Carnegie Commission on Higher Education, *Quality and Equality: New Levels of Federal Responsibility for Higher Education,* (Berkeley: By the Commission, December 1968); U.S. Dept. of Health, Education and Welfare, *Toward a Long-Range Plan for Federal Support for Higher Education: A Report to the President* (Washington, D.C.: U.S. Government Printing Office, January 1969); and Ronald A. Wolk, *Alternative Methods of Federal Funding for Higher Education* (Berkeley: Carnegie Commission on Higher Education, 1968).

[4]For an explanation of this idea, see *Educational Opportunity Bank,* A Report of the Panel on Educational Innovation to the U.S. Commissioner of Education, the Director of the National Science Foundation, and the Special Assistant to the President for Science and Technology, August, 1967.

[5]State Board of Regents, *Freedom to Pursue a College Education,* (Albany: The University of the State of New York, August, 1967).

Bibliography

I. Historical Development of the Community Colleges

Brick, Michael. "The Development of Higher Education in the United States," in *The World Yearbook of Education, 1971-72*. London: Evans Brothers Ltd., 1971.

Butts, R. Freeman, and Cremin, Lawrence A. *A History of Education in American Culture*. New York: Henry Holt & Co., 1953.

Eells, Walter C. *The Junior College*. Boston: Houghton Mifflin Co., 1931.

Fields, Ralph F. *The Community College Movement*. New York: McGraw-Hill Book Co., 1962.

Koos, Leonard V. *The Junior-College Movement*. Boston: Ginn & Co., 1925.

Seashore, Carl E. *The Junior College Movement*. New York: Henry Holt & Co., 1940.

II. Financing Higher Education

Benson, Charles S. *The Economics of Public Education*, 2nd ed. Boston: Houghton Mifflin Co., 1961.

Carnegie Commission on Higher Education. *Quality and Equality: New Levels of Federal Responsibility for Higher Education*. Berkeley: By the Commission, December, 1968.

Cheit, Earl F. *The New Depression in Higher Education*. New York: McGraw-Hill Book Co., 1971.

Coons, John E.; Clune, William H., III; and Sugarman, Stephen D. *Private Wealth and Public Education*. Cambridge: Harvard University Press, The Belknap Press, 1970.

Friedman, Milton. *Capitalism and Freedom*. Chicago: University of Chicago Press, 1962.

Garms, Walter I. "The Prediction of State-Local Expenditures for Higher and Lower Education in the United States," in Robert D. Leiter, ed., *Costs and Benefits of Higher Education.* Boston: Twayne Publishers, 1975.

Joint Economic Committee of the Congress. *The Economics and Financing of Higher Education in the United States.* Washington, D.C.: U.S. Government Printing Office, 1969.

National Commission on the Financing of Postsecondary Education. *Financing Postsecondary Education in the United States.* Washington, D.C.: By the Commission, December 1968.

New York State Board of Regents. *Freedom to Pursue a College Education.* Albany: The University of the State of New York, August 1967.

Second Newman Report: National Policy and Higher Education. Cambridge: M.I.T. Press, 1973.

U.S. Department of Health, Education, and Welfare. *Toward a Long-Range Plan for Federal Support for Higher Education: A Report to the President.* Washington, D.C.: U.S. Government Printing Office, January 1969.

Wolk, Ronald A. *Alternative Methods of Federal Funding for Higher Education.* Berkeley: Carnegie Commission on Higher Education, 1968.

III. The Effects of Education on Individuals

Averch, Harvey A., et al. *How Effective is Schooling? A Critical Review and Synthesis of Research Findings.* Santa Monica: Rand Corporation, 1972.

Becker, Gary S., *Human Capital.* New York: National Bureau of Economic Research, 1964.

Bowles, Samuel, and Levin, Henry M. "The Determinants of Scholastic Achievement—An Appraisal of Some Recent Evidence," *Journal of Human Resources,* vol. 3, no. 1 (Winter 1968), pp. 3-24.

Coleman, James S., et al. *Equality of Educational Opportunity.* Washington, D.C.: U.S. Government Printing Office, 1966.

Garms, Walter I. "A Benefit-Cost Analysis of the Upward Bound Program," *Journal of Human Resources,* vol. 6, no. 2 (Spring 1971), pp. 206-220.

Guthrie, James W., et al. *Schools and Inequality.* Cambridge: M.I.T. Press, 1971.

Jencks, Christopher, et al. *Inequality: A Reassessment of the Effect of Family and Schooling in America.* New York: Basic Books, 1972.

Index